Library of
Davidson College

GROWING UP HASIDIC

Immigrant Communities & Ethnic Minorities
in the United States & Canada: 6

[ISSN 0749-5951]

GROWING UP HASIDIC

Education and Socialization
in the Bobover Hasidic Community

Robert Mark Kamen

AMS PRESS
NEW YORK

Library of Congress Cataloging in Publication Data
Kamen, Robert Mark.
  Growing up Hasidic.

  (Immigrant Communities & Ethnic Minorities in the United States & Canada, ISSN 0749-5951; 6)
    Bibliography: p.
    Includes index.
    1. Hasidim—New York (N.Y.)—Social life and customs. 2. Jews—New York (N.Y.)—Social Life and customs. 3. Brooklyn (New York, N.Y.)—Social Life and customs. I. Title. II. Title: Bobover Hasidic community. III. Series.
F128.9.J5K36 1985   305.6'96'074723   83-45358
ISBN 0-404-19411-7

COPYRIGHT © 1985 by AMS PRESS, INC.
All rights reserved

Manufactured in the United States of America

Contents

Acknowledgments	ix
Introduction	1
CHAPTER I	13
A wedding; immigration: promises and problems; the Hasidic Community of Boro Park	
CHAPTER II	32
Community consolidation; a typical school day; a child's first audience with The Rebbe; pre-school education, nursery and kindergarten; Chayder	
CHAPTER III	74
Coming of age: pre-mesivta and mesivta; emergence of the peer group	
CHAPTER IV	93
Betrothal; employment objectives and opportunities	
APPENDIX I	109
Secular education	
APPENDIX II	124
The questionnaire as a research tool	
Genealogy	128
Glossary	129
Bibliography	133
Index	135

For My Grandfather
ABE MORGENSTEIN

ACKNOWLEDGMENTS

The bulk of the information for this paper was not derived from books found on library shelves, or diaries whose writers are long dead. Rather, it was gathered from among members of a living, thriving community. It is not an easy task for a stranger to drop into the midst of a society and begin poking and probing about. Nor is it any easier for the people, whose daily lives are suddenly the object of another's curiosity, to respond willingly and honestly to questions of a personal as well as an impersonal nature.

Therefore, I would like to take this opportunity to thank all the members of the Bobover Community for their patience and kindness in tolerating my intrusion into their lives; there are too many people to thank personally. However, I would like to extend my appreciation to the Bobover Rov, the Rebbetzen, their sons and daughters for the immeasurable courtesy they extended to me on numerous occasions. Their willingness to receive me in their homes and at their celebrations greatly facilitated my acceptance in the community-at-large. I would also like to thank Rabbi Moishe Kessler, the principal of the Yeshiva, his Rebbetzen and family for their help. Despite a sixteen hour work day, Rabbi Kessler was always available to answer questions, arrange interviews and generally "smooth over the way." Also, I would like to thank Rabbi Z.M. Lichtig whose mere presence first fired my interest in Hasidim.

Finally, I would like to thank the students and teachers of the Bobover Yeshiva, from the youngest to the oldest, for their enthusiasm and willingness to help a stranger in their midst.

R.M.K.

INTRODUCTION

As a child growing up in New York City, I would occasionally pass through certain sections of Brooklyn where the Hasidim[1] had settled and reorganized their communities. For a child it was always fascinating to see these people on the streets of New York in their exotic garb: the men in wide-brimmed black hats, long black coats buttoned right to left, with bearded faces and long side curls; the women in long-sleeved, high-necked dresses, winter or summer. They were Jews from Eastern Europe who had immigrated, possibly from the same towns as my own grandparents, shortly after the second World War. But unlike my grandparents and the immigrants before them, the Hasidim refused to abandon their own customs for newer, American, ways. They lived, I was told, by the same cultural and religious standards as they had in Europe. Since they rarely had any social contact outside their own communities, little was known about their lives here in the United States. My grandparents could recount stories based on events they had heard about or seen as teenagers in Europe, but they knew almost nothing about the Hasidic community in New York City.

Hasidism, as a movement, began in the eighteenth

century in response to the gloom and disorientation brought about by a period of Jewish massacres and false Messianic hopes which left East European Jewry physically and spiritually exhausted. The founder of this new movement, Israel Baal Shem Tov, preached redemption through personal experience of God. He minimized the importance of scholarly pursuits and extolled sincerity and inner piety as the keys to enlightenment. At the center of this philosophy was an optimism which attempted to counteract the general despondency prevalent through Eastern European Jewish communities. The movement's popularity spread rapidly after the death of the Baal Shem Tov in 1760, and of his successor, Dov Baer, in 1772. The men who acquired their Hasidic beliefs as disciples of these two moved throughout Eastern Europe, establishing centers and attracting followers. These <u>tzaddikim</u> (righteous men) and their successors were an integral part of the success Hasidim enjoyed among the masses. As tzaddikim, these first <u>Rebbes</u> (masters) stood as intermediaries between God and man. Possessed with mystical powers, they could intercede in Heaven on behalf of mankind. This idea, and the personal charismatic nature of these Rebbes, drew people to the Hasidic "courts." That a Hasid could travel to the court of his Rebbe, leave his worldly troubles at the gates, join in a fellowship of joy and prayer, confide his problems to someone capable of influencing his fate, appealed to many.

Dynasticism became another force in the growth and perpetuation of Hasidism. The tzaddik as possessor of a "higher soul" was also believed to possess "holy seed." This concept of hereditary saintliness allowed sons to succeed fathers as Rebbes. The stability which grew out of this situation helped strengthen local tradition and establish each Hasidic center as a world unto itself. With the Rebbe at the head, surrounded by his court, Hasidism became fixed around individuals rather than locations. It was the charisma of the Rebbe that provided a focus. If a Rebbe moved, his court was sure to follow.

The Hasidic world view derives from a centuries-old Jewish tradition. The four basic components of this identity are: God, <u>Torah</u>, Israel, and the belief in messianic deliverance. God is incorporeal, subject to neither time nor space. Torah, the Pentateuch or Five Books of Moses, composed before the creation of the world, was not revealed to mankind until Moses received them on Mount Sinai. In a broader sense of the world, Torah may refer to all Jewish religious writings in addition to the Pentateuch, from the time of the Prophets to the present. Although the Pentateuch stands alone as the purest statement of divine will and purpose, Prophets and other writings which along with the Pentateuch comprise the Jewish Bible are also believed to stem from revelation, albeit of a rather less divine nature. _Talmud_ exists as a counterpart of the Torah. Supposedly orally transmitted from Moses to the time of its compilation, which ended around 400 A.D., the Talmud explains in detail the general laws revealed in the Torah. Talmud is not based on direct revelation, but it is believed that its compilation was aided by an affinity with God's Holy Spirit. Commentaries from the completion of Talmud to the present time are technically considered Torah, but of a lower and finite order. The identity of Israel as a nation, dispersed, yet united, a people with allegiance to a concept rather than a physical boundary, draws its sustenance from this perception of Torah. At Sinai, God gave the Jews Torah, or divine purpose. The Jews were chosen, it is believed, to uphold Torah because they alone among nations possessed souls capable of this awesome burden. Their birthright and hence, their identity with Israel cannot be renounced. In addition, it is believed that all souls of all generations were present at Sinai when Torah was accepted from God. The acceptance of Torah and, consequently, Jewish identity, is irrevocable.

By accepting Torah, Jews entered into a covenant with God. In return for obeying the laws of Torah, Israel would be led to the Holy Land, blessed with a peaceful life in this world, and eternal life in the next. In addition to the specifications for man's correct behavior towards both his fellow men and God that are part of the Torah, the Jews have been provided with a continuous succession of divinely inspired leaders from Moses and the first Prophets, to Talmudic and post-Talmudic sages, such as the Baal Shem Tov and his disciples, to the rabbinical luminaries of the present day. Jews, however, have periodically disregarded both this covenant and their spiritual leaders, and their fate has been one of suffering, wandering, and persecution. Despite their deviance, God's word remains. The Jews, as a nation, will repossess the Holy land with the coming of the God-sent Messiah, and the universe shall know eternal harmony.[2]

Initially, Hasidim could be seen only in the Williamsburg section of Brooklyn. But as the groups grew, several new areas in Brooklyn and outside the city limits became centers for Hasidic life. Such expansion denotes a sharp increase in the Hasidic population, and since most Hasidic groups do not actively proselytize, whatever growth that has occurred has come from within the community itself. This being the situation, it is essential to community continuity and expansion that subsequent generations should not be drawn away and assimilated into the American culture which surrounds them. The experiences of the various groups in America are similar in one respect: in the thirty years since Hasidim first began immigrating here community membership has soared from a handful of families to several thousand in the larger groups. How has this been accomplished? How does a community whose existence is determined by strictly defined religious and cultural boundaries survive and flourish in the midst of a social environment such as the New York metropolis?

This study is an attempt to answer the above question. The results reported below are based on fieldwork carried out from 1972 through 1974 in the educational facility of the Bobover Hasidim of Boro Park, Brooklyn. The goal of this research was to describe the organization of the educational system, the major beliefs and assumptions on which it is based, and the way in which it is experienced in the lives of young people passing through it.

Since 1961, when the first in depth study of an American Hasidic community appeared, social scientists have carried out relatively little research among the Hasidim; the two major studies available on Hasidic life in the United States, both conducted in Williamsburg among Hasidim of Hungarian origin, pay little attention to the educational system.[3] The Bobover Hasidic group, whose educational system is described here, originated in the town of Bobov, Grybow county in western Galicia, now part of Poland. It represents the largest group of Galician Hasidim living in the United States today.

The fact that the Bobover community was founded only a little more than one hundred years ago by the grandfather of the present Rebbe (see genealogy) does not conflict with their world view. The Bobover Hasidim see themselves as part of an elite continuum; they are direct descendants of the men and women who received the law on Mount Sinai. Like their ancestors, they are committed to obeying the precepts of the Law. "In order to keep the commandments, you must first know them. The better you know them, the better you can keep them....There is so much to know, two lifetimes is not enough. There is always something else to learn. This is why we never stop learning, learning never stops."[4]

A male child officially enters the educational system before his fifth birthday and continues attending eight or nine hours of classes daily until marriage at age twenty or twenty one. The Yeshiva becomes his world; its population his behavioral models. Therefore, it is considered imperative that a cohesive, well-directed educational system be maintained, one that operates in complete consonance with the ideals of the group.

The present study attempts to describe the setting and organized patterns of behavior in which socialization takes place, i.e. the "phenomenal culture." Secondly, it attempts to describe the ideational culture which lies behind it, that is the conceptual "standards for perceiving, believing, evaluating and acting."[5] In order to explore the ideational as well as the phenomenal culture, I applied a basic field study methodology employing the techniques of participant observation and informal interviews supplemented by key informant interviews. By balancing my own observation of what I heard and saw in the environment with the explanations and perceptions from several key informants, I tried to construct a comprehensive description of what was happening and why it was happening.[6]

In addition to recording the world view of the Bobover community and day to day life in Boro Park as it applies to the educational system, I also wanted to present a more personal documentation of the educational experience as it is actually lived by the people themselves. To determine what the personal experience is like required intensive interviews with people from every age group, for very often time clouded emotions and erased the feelings experienced at a significant occasion; yet, at other times, temporal distance from an event placed it in a clearer perspective. I also attended numerous ceremonies, and sat in daily classes to observe emotions and actions first-hand. My goal in this was to bring a more personal focus to bear on the community under examination. In order to convey more authentic feeling and emotion, traditional analyses have been supplemented, at times, with descriptive narrative.

I began to visit Boro Park in the fall of 1972. My initial introduction into the Bobover community was through the Principal and administrator of the Yeshiva, Rabbi Moishe Kessler. This proved to be fortuitous. Hasidim are extremely concerned that their children's environment not be "contaminated" by overexposure to secular influences. And the presence of a stranger in the Yeshiva, where the students are supposed to be surrounded by Torah and the highest religious principles, would never be tolerated by the community. However, with Rabbi Kessler's aid I was allowed certain privileges normally denied to any outsider except City and State school inspectors. At first interviews were arranged for me with older students and a few young men who worked in the Yeshiva. I was taken by Rabbi Kessler to specific classrooms and allowed to observe parts of daily lessons. I was expected to report to the administrative offices when I entered the building and when I left. As time passed and I became a more familiar presence in the Yeshiva, these restrictions were relaxed. I was able to come and go as I pleased and could talk to any member of the Yeshiva population who would talk to me. Class visits, however, had to be arranged beforehand by Rabbi Kessler despite the fact that I had spoken with many of the children and young men who occupied the classes. The teachers in the Yeshiva, being mostly members of the community, feel a special responsibility for their students. As teachers they must exemplify the attitudes and beliefs they impart. Shielding the children from unnecessary and potentially disconcerting secular influences is as much a part of a teacher's responsibility as is imparting subject matter. Therefore, it was always necessary for Rabbi Kessler to "smooth the way" for my entrance into any classroom. After class hours I always attempted to interview the Rabbi I had observed that day. Some consented to answer questions, as well as ask a few of their own. Some refused to speak to me at all, thereby expressing disapproval. The student population was more cooperative. Initially they were hesitant to engage in conversations that extended beyond polite, but curt, answers. It was suspected, I was later told, that I represented one of the administrative agencies which regularly sent inspectors to report on conditions in both the educational and administrative functioning of the Yeshiva. However, once the confidence of a few boys was gained, I was besieged by informants as eager to question me as I was to question them. I became accepted as "the guy who's writing a book on Bobov" and had to limit my interviews to a selected group of key informants in order to collect manageable data.[7]

While the bulk of the information used in this study was obtained through observation and interviews, I also administered a questionnaire to 200 students which was structured to elicit information in three areas. While the results were not completely satisfactory, it did allow me to reach a larger proportion of the student population and to supplement information obtained in other ways.[8]

Footnotes - Introduction

1. Hebrew or Yiddish words are underlined the first time they appear.

2. For a more detailed discussion of the Hasidic belief system, see Israel Rubin, *Satmar: An Island in the City*. Quadrangle Books, Chicago, 1972.

3. Solomon Poll, *The Economic Organization of a Religious Community* (Ph.D. dissertation, Department of Sociology, University of Pennsylvania, 1961).

4. All quotations which appear below, unless noted otherwise, are attributed to members of the Bobover Hasidic Community.

5. Ward Goodenough, *Description and Comparison in Cultural Anthropology*. Aldine, Chicago, 1970, p. 104.

6. Pertti J. Pelto, *Anthropological Research: The Structure of Inquiry*. Harper and Row, New York, 1970, p. 93.

7. Pelto, p. 90.

8. For a description of the questionaire, its validity and limitations, see Appendix II.

CHAPTER I

The groom is nervous. His eyes are glazed and watery. He has been rocking back and forth since he sat down in the center of the long table. From time to time he strokes his wispy first beard as if to verify its existence. The shtreiml, with its wide sable brim and flat black crown, covers his close-cropped head. His new white shirt is buttoned stiffly at the collar. The black silk kapota, hanging to his knees, shimmers with his constant swaying.

The table before him is filled with honey cake, small paper cups and bottles of whiskey. He gazes neither at the food and drink, nor away. He has not eaten all day. To his left and right sit his father and father-in-law. Past them, respectively, grandfathers, uncles, cousins, brothers and friends. They are all dressed the same as the groom. The older men have thicker beards, and some have their peyes, the traditional side curls, pushed behind their ears. The table is lively from one end to the other with men talking, drinking, singing, and laughing. It seems that except for the father and father-in-law, no one is paying much heed to the anxious groom.

Young children in bright-colored clothes with long

dangling peyes dance around the table, trying to snare a piece of the sweet, fresh cakes. Songs and toasts break out spontaneously, the volume swelling as they are picked up by the group.

Down the hallway, in another room, sitting on a raised platform against one wall, the bride looks out over a crowd of attentive relatives and friends. To the left and right of her "throne" stand her mother and mother-in-law. She is pale from fasting, but smiling and joking with the crowd of well wishers. The women are dressed fashionably but modestly; arms, necks, and knees are covered. The married women are wearing highly styled <u>sheytl</u> (wigs) while the unmarried girls have their hair plainly styled or severely pulled back, held by pins or a bow.

A band is playing lively East European folk songs and the girls are dancing in a wide circle around the crowd and the platform. The floor directly before the bride clears and several young girls break from the circle and dance towards her. They sing well-wishes for the future, and implore her to join them in one last dance as a girl. She laughingly refuses and stays seated on her "throne."

Four men hold the long wooden standards as the cloth <u>chuppa</u>, the wedding canopy, flaps in the chilled December air. The groom, his father, his father-in-law, and an old man with a resplendent white beard and sparkling blue eyes stand beneath the chuppa. All around them in the dark, shifting figures move and rub their hands to stave off the cold. The groom sways to and fro, his eyes closed, his lips forming silent prayers.

All at once the circle breaks and the men move to one side. The darkness is broken by the flicker of a clutch of candles; with the light to the groom's side, comes the bride. She is led around the groom in a circle seven times. Her veil is so thick that her mother and mother-in-law must carefully guide her in her steps. As the last circling is completed, they place her by the groom's side, and with their braided candles, retreat to where the other women have joined the circle.

Several older men step forward and give their blessings to the couple. The ceremony is short. The marriage contract is read, the blessings are given. A glass is placed under a white cloth. The groom crushes it zealously, releasing a good deal of his tension. The couple is led to a private room where they will spend their first minutes alone, as prescribed by the Law.

The chuppa folds from the center as the poles are lowered. The men and women, anxious to leave the cold behind, hurry back to their respective halls for the wedding feast.

In the men's hall, the long dinner tables have been cleared away, and the open area is filled with whirling shtreiml and kapota. The men have joined hands in a large circle and are moving rapidly around the hall. In the center of the circle several younger men are performing acrobatic feats. One man dances with a bottle on his head, and a plate precariously balanced atop the bottle. Another is balancing several chairs on an outstretched palm. Some of the younger boys form a human pyramid, while others execute flips in mid-air. The old men sit along the walls singing, clapping gleefully, taking delight in the antics of their sons and grandsons. Occasionally they will move out onto the floor when the music's tempo dies down, to circle slowly, gracefully, arms outstretched, eyes closed.

In the women's hall, the dancing is more subdued, but still lively. Everyone wants to dance with the bride. Distant relatives and friends form a large circle around the immediate family, while they, in turn, dance arm-in-arm around the bride. One at a time the women closest to the bride enter the center to dance a few brief turns with her. The outer circle soon closes and the bride accepts the embraces and compliments of everyone. Even the oldest grandmother present finds the strength to dance at least one slow turn with the bride.

The music has died down to a waltz. The bride, surrounded by her immediate family, sits at the entrance to the men's hall. The floor has been cleared. The men are sitting at the hall's far end, lining the walls. The party has thinned, with the discreet departure of all but the closest friends and relatives. As the bride's father walks across the hall even the whispers in the crowd are quelled; the band's tempo slows, the volume subsides. The bride rises and grasps the corner of a white handkerchief her father has extended. Gently he leads her through her first dance steps with a man, the handkerchief held taut between them. There is marked silence in the hall, where only moments before a seemingly endless tumult ensued, as father and daughter dip and glide gracefully to the waltz's flow.

The dancers circle the floor once, twice; the father drawing the daughter closer to her groom. Until finally in an instant it is the groom holding one end of the handkerchief, the bride holding the other. Whispers break past bearded lips, hands mop the sweat from under sable brims. The women smile and wipe at their tears. In a corner, two little girls dance to the waltz, a handkerchief between them.

The bride is smiling and blushing deeply. The groom can manage only a nervous grin. The wedding is over. For each of the following seven nights, the young couple will attend <u>shevas bruchas</u> (seven blessings) parties in their honor held in a different home each night. For a year they will be considered newlyweds. And except for those times when he is at work, prayer, or study, the young husband is expected to spend all his time with his bride. Like her married relatives and friends, the bride will now wear a wig whenever she is seen in public. The groom, like all married men, will be seen in his shtreiml on holidays and the Sabbath. At prayer, he will now be privileged to wear a _talis_, the fringed prayer shawl. They will set up housekeeping, have children, participate fully in community affairs; perpetuating the credo and belief of a culture that began nearly three-hundred years ago in the Carpathian mountains of Eastern Europe.

What I have been describing is a traditional wedding celebration as it is observed among the Hasidic communities of New York City.[1] Marriage among the Hasidim, as in any small, autonomous population, is a particularly significant event.[2] For it heralds the imminent existence of another generation to perpetuate the beliefs and values that distinguish the group from the homogeneity of the majority culture.

To Hasidim, the marriage ceremony is the culmination of a series of events which serve to signify the passage from childhood to adulthood, and full acceptance into the community. For with marriage, the young couple will begin to participate in the lifestyle for which their upbringing has prepared them: to raise a family according to Judaic and Hasidic tradition.

Hasidim first appeared in this country in significant numbers only after World War II. Of an estimated two million Hasidim living throughout Eastern Europe before 1940, only a handful survived the holocaust of war and the concentration camps. Some groups, like the Hasidim of Hungary, who had managed to avoid persecution until 1943, emerged relatively intact.[3] But other groups, particularly the courts of Poland and Galicia, were so decimated that recovery seemed unlikely. And for many courts, whose entire leadership had perished, distinction passed to history.

Memories of the holocaust, and the emerging communist governments made resettlement an impossibility for the courts. The countries of Western Europe, struggling to rebuild shattered economies and populations, could not absorb large numbers of refugees. Palestine was still a British Mandate, but the clouds of inevitable conflict were, by 1946, already gathering. And although some Hasidim did immigrate to Palestine, the majority shied away from the possibility of more strife and violence, and opted for a more stable situation.

So the United States, by virtue of the facts that it had emerged from the war economically and politically intact and had a large, affluent Jewish population which enjoyed equal rights of citizenship, became the regrouping point for the displaced courts. Pockets of Hasidim remained in Europe, mostly in Belgium and England. But New York City, with the largest Jewish community in the non-communist world, became the center of Hasidic activity and culture after World War II.

If the United States with its history of political and religious liberties and its economic opportunities offered the promise of regeneration to a confused and decimated culture, it also presented the spectre of assimilation into the secular world. This was its reputation. Many of the new immigrants feared that what the death camps began, life in America would finish.

> Believe me, I was not so happy to come here. But, of course, there was no place else to go. And when I came here, for the first few years when there was nothing for religious Jews, nothing like we had in Europe, and the Rov was trying to make something, I only worried that my sons shouldn't grow up to think that the things they saw in America, New York City, were right for a Jew.

This fear of assimilation, the alienation of the next generation from the traditional culture of the parents, is not peculiar to the Hasidim, nor is it unfounded. Since the Pilgrims and Puritans fled England to settle the New England coastline, immigrant groups of varying religious denominations have attempted to establish and order their communities so as to maintain cohesion within their own cultural boundaries, despite the pressure and persistence of secular, external influence.

For instance, between 1905 and 1907, nearly five thousand Molokans, a group of Russians whose deviation from the Orthodox Church had resulted in persecution and ultimate exile, established several communities in southern California. By 1932, however, these communities were rapidly assimilating into the surrounding population.[4]

More recently, the problems of assimilation among the Amish and Mennonite communities of Pennsylvania, Ohio, and Iowa, whose forebears first settled in Germantown, Pennsylvania in 1683, have been brought to the public attention through numerous studies and multimedia presentations. Both groups depend heavily on literal physical separation to control what they consider assimilative influences. But because of their opposition, on religious grounds, to certain aspects of modern technology, their futures as autonomous communities depend on the viability of maintaining profitable, pre-industrial agrarian lives in a technologically aggressive society.

In the history of pietist settlement in the United States, the Hasidim of New York City are unique in their determination to remain autonomous in the midst of a metropolitan environment whose agencies and functioning social institutions are contrary to the beliefs and values espoused by Hasidic culture.

Unlike the Amish, Mennonite, or Hutterite communities, the Hasidim have not chose physical separation as their strategy for coping with assimilation. It is true that in 1961, one of the courts, the Skverer Hasedim, originally from the Ukrainian town of Skvira, established a residential community north of New York City, just outside the town of Spring Valley. The settlement, an incorporated village, is called New Skver. However, the Skverer still maintain close economic and social ties to the "contaminating" cultural environment of New York City. And the vast majority of the Hasidic population remains where it has been for the past three decades, in several sections of the borough of Brooklyn.

Boro Park is located in the southwest section of Brooklyn, ten minutes by car from lower Manhattan. Its boundaries extend from Ocean Parkway south to 60th Street, and from 9th Avenue east to 18th Avenue. Along Ocean Parkway, the buildings tend to be taller, some with terraces that afford a view of the lower Manhattan skyline on clear days. Farther south, the buildings are smaller, rising no more than five stories. There are many large, turn-of-the-century houses which necessity has subdivided into apartments. In recent years, the trend towards constructing two-story, four-family garden apartments has kept the skyline and the atmosphere of the area more residential and less urban.

There is no heavy industry in Boro Park, so traffic tends to be light, restricted to residents' cars or people passing through to neighboring Flatbush or Bensonhurst. The stores that line the commercial avenues depend upon local retail trade. Besides two chain supermarkets, there are several well-stocked groceries, as well as fresh produce stands, drugstores, dry good stores, dry-cleaners, and bakeries.

Before the mid-sixties, the population of the neighborhood was composed mainly of second generation Jewish and Italian families. There were some Hasidim, but they represented only a fraction of the Jewish population, which was divided between the Orthodox and Conservative branches of Judaism. Some congregations were more observant than others, and while a <u>yarmulka</u> (skull-cap) was not an uncommon sight in Boro Park, the general appearance of Jew and Gentile alike was indistinguishable. All this changed in 1966.

The overwhelming majority of the seven hundred families which comprise the Bobover Hasidic community live close to the Bobover Rov, Shlomo Halberstam, in Boro Park. Most members of the community acknowledge that although it is not the best place to be living, it is certainly preferable to the Williamsburg or Crown Heights sections, both heavily populated by Hasidim, where the rapid deterioration of the neighborhood has brought a dramatic rise in crime.[5]

The Bobover Rov came to New York from London, where in 1946 it was agreed by the surviving members of the community that he succeed his father, the late Ben Zion Halberstam, as head of the court. With the aid of friends and established agencies, two buildings were purchased on West 85th Street in Manhattan to serve as a receiving center for Jewish refugees and orphans as they arrived from Europe. Word quickly spread through orthodox Jewish immigrant communities here, and displaced persons centers in Europe, that the Bobover Rov had settled in New York.

Naturally, many of those who came to the West Side center were Hasidim whose families had followed the Rov's father and grandfather in Europe. But significant numbers of Hasidim whose own leaders had been exterminated came to see the Rov as well. Since the Rov was one of the few Polish Rebbes to survive the war he became the focal point for many Polish and Galician Hasidim whose own leadership had perished.

When my parents first came to this country

they lived with my mother's cousin. My father was unhappy. There was nobody he could relate to, as a friend. He had grown his beard back after the war and tried to live as a religious Jew. But in Providence, even though there were people who said they were Jews, it was hard. After all, my family had followed the Bobover all the way from the beginning, when the Rov's grandfather was Rov in Auschpitzien.

So my father heard through a letter that the Bobover Rov was in New York. And, of course, he became very excited. After all, Hasidus is a whole way of life, not just a small thing.

So one week he went to New York to see the Rov. It was the summer and he went to where the Rov was, on the West Side. There were two buildings: one was a dormitory and a Besh medresh, like a Yeshiva, and the other one was being used to train people for different jobs like watch repair, sewing, diamond work. My father sat and talked with the Rov. He told him, I suppose, how he was afraid that in America he and his sons would lose yiddischkeit forever. The Rov said it was his purpose to remake Bobov and a place for Hasidus in America. He told my father to move down to New York City and not to worry. In one month we were living here and my father became a butcher.

Within a few years, the situation for many of the immigrants stabilized, and the need for a more permanent social arrangement than existed on the West Side became evident. In 1954, when the Rov and his family moved to Crown Heights in Brooklyn, the families of his court followed. The settlement in Crown Heights was the first attempt at establishing a cohesive community since the dispersion of the Bobover in 1939.

But by the early 1960's, the situation in Crown Heights began changing. Assaults on community members increased. Vandalism was committed in and around the Yeshiva. In 1966 the Rov moved again, this time to Boro Park, and a large portion of the community naturally followed.

The Bobover, although the largest, were by no means the only group of Hasidim to relocate in Boro Park. The same deterioration that occurred in Crown Heights also occurred in Williamsburg, the center of Hasidic life in New York. And several smaller congregations, following the Bobover's lead, found the area more suitable for their families. Shteiblich (prayer rooms) and small Hasidic Yeshivas opened throughout the neighborhood. The appearance of the shtreiml, bekesher, and long, curled peyes soon ceased to draw the attention of longtime residents. And Yiddish was frequently heard in the streets and stores.

Many stores began to stock merchandise that appealed to Hasidic needs and tastes. Several groceries and bakeries, which had previously catered to the Orthodox community, rearranged their standards to comply with the even more stringent guidelines demanded by Hasidim. Businesses that closed on Saturday in accordance with Jewish custom, but opened on Sunday, found their clientele growing.[6]

Although the Hasidic population of Boro Park is significant, in no way does it compose a majority.

Consequently, there are aspects of life in the area that are beyond Hasidic control. Secular influences are still pervasive and easily accessible to Hasidim. Movie theaters are within walking distance of the Yeshivas; corner candy stores sell newspapers and magazines which are not for Hasidic consumption. Non-Hasidic adolescents flirt and court in typical American fashion, holding hands and kissing on the streets. And Manhattan, where many of the Bobover young men and increasing numbers of young women work each day, is only twenty minutes away by public transportation.

The generation now coming of age was not born in Europe; unlike their parents, they have no previous experience to compare with life in New York. Hasidim, as a rule, marry at 19 or 20 years of age; girls are often younger. So the young parents of the community have been born and raised in full exposure to an alternative, and potentially alluring, lifestyle. But with rare exception, they chose to remain in the community, and raise their children according to Hasidic tradition.[7]

How is it accomplished? There is no physical barrier that prevents a child from observing or indulging in activities contrary to community sanctions. Nor is there an economic barrier, such as the Hutterites have attempted to maintain, which limits the individual's contacts with secular society.[8] Even the peculiarities of Hasidic garb no longer function as an exclusionary mechanism. In European society, the distinctive Hasidic dress marked a person with an identity which was cause enough for exclusion from the majority culture. But in the United States, particularly in the metropolitan areas, where identification with a specific group or belief system is not a deterrent from participation in public life, Hasidic dress functions mainly on a level of personal identification.

There are two dominant sources from which Hasidic social organization can be traced. First, there is Torah. Traditionally, Torah has always been the central force in Jewish life. In Torah, exact and explicit directions governing every conceivable aspect of human behavior are presented. Among Orthodox Jewish communities, such as the Hasidim, status is based neither upon wealth nor physical attributes, but on knowledge of and devotion to the precepts of Torah and its attendant commentaries. As noted in the introduction, Torah as a basis for action is a universal trait inherent in all Jewish communities; the transcription is so carefully undertaken that not a letter has been altered from the original documents recorded at Sinai. But since events to which the dispersed nation of Israel has been subjected do not reflect the timelessness of Torah, adaptation has become an intrinsic element in Jewish history. Rabbinical commentary and opinion exist to clarify the generalities of Law, enabling the Jewish population to adhere to its beliefs and values while adjusting to what may seem to be adverse social conditions. Definition of the Law, therefore, is often dictated by the times. The cultural peculiarities which distinguish, for example, a Polish Jew and a Moroccan Jew, can be attributed to a flexibility of the Law, and not a perversion of it. Hence, while Torah is seen as the primary source for much of what exists in the Bobover community today, the specific characteristics of Hasidic society are a result of Judaic adaptation to a particular environment--in this case, Eastern Europe. Over time, the two variables have become so interwoven as to be indistinguishable; religious observance is a combination of both religious and cultural elements.

In the United States, the primary concern among the Bobover has been to establish a strong social and educational facility which will fulfill the needs of community members without compromising the basic tenets of Torah or Hasidic culture. Keenly aware of the ease with which other immigrant groups have dissolved into the mass culture, leaving only token structures or written records of their existence, the Bobover have concentrated on developing a system of enculturation which completely involves the child in community life, forging his identity to that of the community so firmly that, as he grows older and establishes himself as an adolescent and an adult, capable of making decisions for himself and his family, the temptations and allurements of secular American life will seem pallid and unattractive by comparison.

Footnotes - Chapter I

1. Since the courts which comprise the entire Hasidic population originated in various regions of Eastern Europe, some variation in custom and manner of observance can be expected.

2. According to the Bobover Hasidim, there are approximately seven hundred families in the Community.

3. Poll, p. 37.

4. Pauline V. Young, The Pilgrims of Russian Town, University of Chicago Press, Chicago, 1932, p. 2.

5. Jerome Mintz, Legends of the Hasidim, University of Chicago Press, Chicago, 1968, pp. 41-42.

6. Poll, p. 60.

7. There are no accurate records on this subject, due to the reticence of the Hasidim to discuss the subject in anything but the vaguest terms. However, a questionnaire distributed among 200 Yeshiva students provides information to support the fact that rejection of the Hasidic lifestyle is almost non-existent among the Bobover.

8. Lee Emerson Deets, The Hutterites: A Study in Social Cohesion, Ph.D. dissertation, Faculty of Political Science, Columbia University, 1937, pp. 3-7.

CHAPTER II

In Europe, a Rebbe's following was usually not as consolidated as are the contemporary Hasidic communities of New York. The town of Bobov, for instance, where the Bobover Rebbe lived, had a population of 1,422, of which 565 were Jews in 1921.[1] Yet, the Bobover following numbered nearly 10,000 family heads.[2] Hasidim travelled to see their Rebbe. The travelling was an intrinsic element of the Hasidic experience.

> In Europe we would travel for two days to see the Rebbe, so there had to be something important to go to Bobov, not just a small problem. Sometimes my father would go just for <u>Shabbos</u> or <u>yontef</u>. What went on there! People coming from all over. I was only a teenager, but I still remember how it was to travel and then come into Bobov for a Shabbos. It was really something!

The custom of travelling to the Rebbe's court has mostly disappeared among Hasidim today. Except for the satellite communities in Europe, Canada and Israel, most Hasidim live close to their Rebbe in the various sections of Brooklyn. Consolidation of all activity has become a familiar element in the Hasidic experience. To the generation of young adults born in this country whose own children are now attending the Yeshivas, travelling to see the Rebbe exists only in their fathers' reminiscence. Every Shabbos and yontef is spent with the Rebbe. To celebrate a wedding takes a short walk or a car ride. And to attend school from the very first grades until marriage, a Hasid need not leave town, or even his neighborhood. Such consolidation is believed to have facilitated the growth and vitality of the communities existing today.

Among the Bobover, the emphasis placed on the philosophy of consolidation is evident after only a short visit to the community. It is best elucidated by describing a typical day in the life of a nine-year old attending school at the Bobover Yeshiva B'nei Zion.

Classes begin at 8:30 a.m., which means rising at 7:00 to wash, say the morning prayer, eat breakfast, dress and either wait for the school bus or an adult to accompany you to school. Upon entering the Yeshiva, the first thing you see is the Bes Hamedresh, filled since 6:00 with both young and old men. Some of the men are just completing morning prayers and preparing to leave for work; others are seated at long wooden tables where they will remain throughout the day, studying Torah and its commentaries.

The other classrooms are filling with younger and older children, many of whom you know. In your own class you know everybody. And why not? For, with the exception of three or four boys who have transferred from other

Yeshivas, your classmates have been together since the first Chayder. The Rabbi, who is your teacher, enters the room out of breath. He has just deposited his own son in the second grade, two floors below. His peyes are pushed behind his ears. He walks over to Shlomo in the first row and pinches his cheeks as he greets the class. Without removing his hat and coat he pulls out the black <u>Chumesh</u>, and points to the first child in the first row; "Read!" he commands. The day's lessons have begun.

At 12:00 you close your Chumesh and line up with the class to go to lunch. Passing the Bes Hamedresh, which is still full, you see your sister's husband. But the crowd sweeps you down the stairs before you can catch his eye. In the dining hall, you see your brother sitting with your cousin. They are in the third grade together. Lunch is eaten quickly, for it is a sunny day and the Rabbis will allow the classes fifteen or twenty minutes to run around outside.

By 12:45, you are back in your seat with your book open. Lessons begin again and last until 3:00. At 3:00, the Rabbi leaves to continue his own studies in the Bes Hamedresh. For fifteen minutes, classes change and shift, in preparation for "English" studies.[3] Some boys leave it to sit in the Bes Hamedresh and learn with an older student. Their parents do not feel it is necessary or <u>Hasidishe</u> to learn social studies or to read books in English. Arithmetic can be learned at home. At 3:15, the English teacher arrives. "How are you today?" he asks. They are the first English words you have heard all day.

English studies end at 5:30. The building empties quickly, except for the Bes Hamedresh, which is still filled with young men. Your father and your uncle are waiting outside for you and your cousins. The school buses are lined up, blocking traffic on 48th Street. It is only three blocks to your house, and walking after a whole day of sitting feels good.

After dinner you sit and review your lessons with your father. Your brothers are practicing reading prayers together. Since there are no tests in secular subjects this week, there is no need to study them. Evening prayers are recited, and it is time for bed.

The only variation in this schedule is on the Sabbath or certain holidays, when fathers and their sons, mothers and their daughters, congregate in the Bes Hamedresh along with the entire community, to observe the holiday. During the summer, a child either attends the Yeshiva summer school-day program or joins the Bobover summer camp in the Catskill Mountains, where physical activities, such as swimming and hiking, are interspersed with studies.

By consolidating the traditional institutions in one

central location, and by coordinating the activities of the various age groups, a continuous environment has been created for the child, where familiarity and behavioral reinforcement are very high. To achieve this cohesion, and to maintain it over the generations, the Bobover have adapted past practices to meet present needs; they've improvised on their own and "borrowed" certain other ideas, such as nursery or pre-school classes, from the dominant, secular culture.

I

Like many other activities in the Hasidic community, schooling is segregated according to sex. Therefore, it is somewhat confusing, when visiting the Nursery School, to see little boys with yarmulkas covering close-cropped heads and long curling peyes, playing with what appear to be long-tressed little girls. Actually, the visual inconsistency is misleading. For according to Hasidic custom, a male child does not get his first haircut until his third birthday.[4] The "girls," then, are boys whose birthdates do not correspond to the scholastic calendar. And although the educational administration recommends that children do not enter the nursery program until at least their third birthday, the abundance of little shaggy heads reflects the recommendation's flexibility.

Among the Bobover, a male child's first haircut is a significant occasion in which child, parents, grandparents, and siblings all participate with varying degrees of anticipation. Since the first haircutting is performed by the Rov, the attending ritual has perhaps more significance for the gathered adults, who are devoted followers of the Bobover Rov, than for the child. Until this time, the child's conception of the Rov is nebulous. In the course of conversation, the child has come to understand that the Rov is a most respected person. Parents, siblings, and relatives, when speaking of him, do so with awe and reverence. This much the child can understand. Perhaps, while out shopping with his mother, the child has been taken past the Rov's home, a large red brick house that fills the corner of 48th Street where it intersects 15th Avenue, and has had his attention called to the fact that "the Bobover Rebbe lives here, just three blocks from your house." Undoubtedly there will be a picture of the Rov in the home that the child has been shown by his parents. But his grandfather also has a long white beard, and his father wears the same shtreiml on Shabbos. Only the eyes are different--bright and piercing blue--but a child is hardly expected to know such things.

As his third birthday approaches, father, grandfather, and older brothers begin teaching the youngster the Hebrew alphabet. Sometimes a picture book with familiar objects corresponding to each letter is used; in other homes a simple primer with the letters in large and small case serves as a child's first <u>sefer</u> (book). At night, around the dinner table, the father will conduct impromptu tests of the child's progress. Or, in the company of relatives, a grandparent will cajole the child to recite his "Aleph-Bes" (ABC's); candies and kisses reward good performances, mock disappointments accompany poor ones.

If the child is in the Nursery School, he has seen his classmates come to class one day with long tresses like his, and the next day with nearly shaved heads and peyes--and bags of candy for everyone. "The Bobover Rov gave me peyes and put a yarmulka on my head," they will say, "and I read the Aleph-Bes for him."

On the morning of the child's birthday, everyone is up early. The older children have taken the day off from school. The commotion in the house exceeds its usual limits. Everyone is dressed and waiting anxiously while the mother combs and recombs the child's long hair. A few pictures are taken by a family friend or a relative, as the father wraps the child in his black and white striped wool <u>talis</u> and carries him out the door, the whole family following. The child is wrapped in the talis so as to prevent him from seeing anything unholy on this day. The procession arrives at the Rov's house, where it is joined by grandparents, aunts and uncles, the <u>Rebbetzen</u> (the Rebbe's wife), and the Rov's personal secretaries, two burly men with full black beards. There are unopened boxes of cake and bottles of whiskey, accompanied by the ever-present paper cups. The group congregates in a waiting room. The child's face is covered by the silver-braided collar of the talis.

A door opens and the entire entourage files into the Rov's study after the father and child. The men come forward to where the Rov sits behind his desk. He greets each man in turn, shaking hands, smiling, giving blessings. On the wall behind the Rov hangs a finely lettered chart. This is the Rov's <u>Yichus</u>, his family lineage, which extends all the way back to "Duvid Ha-Melech," David, King of Israel. The women gather along the far wall of the room, remaining perfectly still, except for the mother, whose anxious face and nervously moving hands contrast sharply to the quasi-solemnity.

The child meanwhile has been removed from the talis and placed in a chair opposite the Rov, whose full attention has been turned in his direction. He speaks to the child in quiet cheerful tones, spinning a coin to catch the child's eyes. While spinning the coin he sings familiar rhymes, making the child laugh. The men, standing back a few paces, laugh and smile with approval as the Rov continues to devote full attention to the child. A gold pair of scissors appears in the Rov's hand; he shows it to the child and asks if he would like to have his baby's hair cut into the beautiful peyes of a Yeshiva bocher (Yeshiva student). Carefully coached for this moment, the child nods his head, ever so slightly, affirmatively. The Rov now gathers handfulls of hair and begins cutting, all the while talking and singing soothing melodies. Occasionally, the Rov looks up and directs a remark to the men, referring to an appropriate point in Torah or the Talmud. These comments elicit nods and knowing murmurs of agreement. The women have begun to talk among themselves. The mother's eyes are brimming with tears as she watches her baby's curls fall to the floor.

When the cutting is finished, the Rov slips a talis katan, a white cotton vest with four fringed corners, on the child's shoulders, and places a yarmulka on the bare little head. He lifts the child, places him in his father's arms, and wraps them both in a talis. The father kisses his son and gently hands him back to the Rov, wrapped in the talis. The Rov places the child in his lap. An alphabet primer appears on the desk along with a small cup of honey. The Rov opens the primer to the first page, dips his finger into the honey, touches the first letter of the alphabet, and offers the honeyed finger to the child, who licks at it tentatively, "to sweeten his taste for learning Torah." The Rov then begins what is to be the child's first official instruction. He points to the first letter and asks the child what it is. When the child demurs, he pinches his cheeks, coaxing him with a laugh. Parents, grandparents, and assembled relatives silently coax and cajole with their eyes. "Aleph," the Rov says. Weakly, almost inaudibly, the child replies, "Aleph." An expected round of approval encourages the child and he proceeds through the alphabet as the Rov points to each letter.

The recital ends as the Rov pronounces the child fit for learning. He expresses the hope that this generation will grow up in the tradition of Hasidus and Torah, and to see the coming of the Messiah. Parents and relatives crowd the child. Cake and whiskey are passed around, and the traditional toast "L'chaim!" (to life) is extended to all. The mother busies herself collecting the shorn hair, which she will save along with the baby hair of her other sons.

The child is carried in the talis, by his father, down the block to the Yeshiva. He is brought to the first chayder, where the teacher unfolds a large alphabet chart and points to the letters for the child, who, for the second time, recites. "Mazel tov!" (congratulations) yell the young students. They are rewarded for the effort with bags of candy, personally delivered to them by the new Chayder bocher.

Afterwards, the child returns to his own nursery class

where, although the recital is dispensed with, candy and cakes are again distributed. There is status, however short-lived, in the child's memory, associated with this event. He now has peyes, a talis katan, and a yarmulka, the physical identity of a Hasid. He has had his first private audience with the Rov, a fact about which his parents, and the community as a whole, make much ado. And, more important to him perhaps, he has personally treated his classmates to candy and cakes.

The association between the physical markings of a pious Jew, the peyes, the tsitsis, and the yarmulka, and the spiritual mediator between man and God begins with this first encounter of the child with the Rov. It builds with time and experience to become one of the major bonds of the individual and his community. When asked why he wears such things, any Bobover child will respond "because I am a Jew" or "because I am a Hasid." And when asked where he got these things, he invariably answers, "from the Bobover Rov, the Rov gave them to me!"

The nursery school is not a Hasidic tradition. But it has been adopted by the Bobover as a useful precursor to the Chayder which roughly corresponds in age group to the first grade of public school. Since the concept of pre-school was borrowed from the secular culture, the basic format has also been closely followed. As with the American models, the classes are used to provide the child with a more formal approach to learning about the general environment and the basic systems by which society lives. The seasons, the days of the week, the months of the year, numbers, colors, and various objects are all presented in a cohesive system which relies upon group participation, individual recitation and repetition. There are the usual blocks and toys employed during free play periods, and arts and crafts supplies such as crayons, paints, clay, and paste, which are used in conjunction with more specific projects. There is music, mostly on cassette tapes, to which the children will sing along.[5] And the rooms are adorned much like a typical nursery, with pictures and cut-outs identifying the seasons, a holiday, or the more gifted among the class artists. The Hebrew alphabet is taught, but not stressed. Each child learns the letters of his name, and is responsible for identifying his cubbyhole on that basis.

Language, garb, and name, the Bobover maintain, are the three major components in establishing an identity. "These are the three reasons Jews have remained Jews. Since Egypt we have kept these three things in one piece, together like a cloth fabric." Hence, each concept is given priority in the education of the children. First and last names have resisted anglicization. Dress, of course, is strictly regulated. And all instruction and conversation in the school and the home is in Yiddish. In fact, many of the children who attend the Nursery School cannot speak any English, although their parents are quite fluent. On occasion, adults will speak English among themselves, but almost always they will address children in Yiddish. If by chance a child picks up a few words of English, he is discouraged from using them in favor of the Yiddish equivalents.

The children are imbued at an early age with a preference for communicating in Yiddish instead of English, except when absolutely necessary. A child of three who attempts to speak English to his friends is roundly scolded by them for not behaving like a good boy. Whereas a teacher will often compliment children for speaking such "<u>sheyna Yiddish</u>" (beautiful Yiddish).

The laws and mitzvot (good deeds) enunciated in Torah, which comprise the basis for action and behavior in Hasidic society, are explained through song, parable, and example to the Nursery classes. If a child misbehaves or exhibits behavior that is contrary to some basic commandment, the aberration is recounted to the class as being contrary to "right" behavior and compared unfavorably with the ideal.

Periodically, teachers will send a mimeographed sheet home with their students, explaining to the parents that

such-and-such attitude is being instilled in the child.
Asking for cooperation, the teachers will suggest parental
reinforcement every time the child performs this specific
commandment or mitzvah, and also that they send notes to
school along with the child, reporting the frequency with
which such behavior is exhibited. Upon receipt of such notes,
the teachers are quick to praise the child publicly. The
rate of parental compliance is very high.

With the exception of free play, most activities and
lessons in the Nursery are designed to strengthen the child's
associations with Bobover goals and attitudes. This is accomplished by coordinating what can be termed "general"
knowledge with specific, or religious, knowledge. A lesson
on the shapes and colors of fruits extends to instruction
on the blessings one must recite before eating such food, or
even the laws governing when these foods may be eaten.
Since the children come from similar home environments, such
discussions have immediate, rather than abstract, associations. And when a teacher asks how many children comply
with the laws and say a certain blessing, or perform a
special ritual at home, all hands are raised.

Similarly, the stories that are read to the children are
all based on presentation of the particular rather than the
general. Since no English teaching aids are used, most of
the contemporary stories are contrived by the staff. And

interwoven throughout each one is a moral lesson. Other stories draw their substance from Jewish history and Torah. Each one is endowed with ethical, as well as entertaining, qualities.

The numerous Jewish holidays provide a major source of material for the curriculum. The reasons for observances are presented in language and images a child can understand. Arts and crafts projects produce the material objects associated with the particular holiday. Likewise, traditional foods such as <u>hamentaschen</u>, a triangular, fruit-filled cake eaten during the <u>Purim</u> festival, are served along with the daily lunches and snacks. In the case of some holidays like <u>Chanukah</u>, where the observance recounts a glorious exploit in history, class plays, complete with costumes, will be arranged for the children to act out the events that gave rise to the celebration.

The desire to maintain a close association between home and school environments encourages parental participation, not only through impersonal mimeographed directives, but actual physical presence as well. Parents regularly pay impromptu visits to the Nursery and respond eagerly to any request for assistance on the part of the staff. Rather than rely on the bus service the school offers, most mothers and fathers prefer to accompany their children to and from school. It is not uncommon for a parent to arrive at the school shortly before dismissal and chat with the teacher while helping the child dress for the walk home.

Nursery School enrollment is overwhelmingly Hasidic, though not exclusively Bobover. Since most Yeshivas in Boro Park do not have adequate pre-school facilities, many non-Bobover Hasidim opt to send their children to the Bobover Nursery. There are a few non-Hasidic parents who enroll their children in the program primarily because of the emphasis on spoken Yiddish. Despite the fact that they live more integrated lives in American society, there is still a desire to teach their children Yiddish. Their hope is that daily association in school, along with appropriate reinforcement at home, will provide the child with a strong background in the Yiddish language. These children are usually withdrawn from the Bobover Yeshiva system by the first grade, when formal instruction in prayer and Torah begin, and placed in non-Hasidic Yeshivas. The Bobover, for their part, do not encourage the enrollment of non-Hasidic children, preferring to limit access to their facility to Hasidic children. More than likely, non-Hasidic homes will contain objects, such as televisions, and condone behavior contrary to Hasidic beliefs. The Bobover do not want to expose their children to conflicting environments too early in life. "We consider ourselves progressive, yes. But progressive does not mean a change in the way we are living.

What it means is acknowledging that, yes, there is an outside world and yes, certain things do exist that are not Hasidishe, and not for us. There is time enough for a child to learn about the "don'ts"; here, we are concerned with the "do's".

The kindergarten functions as an extension of the Nursery program, with the exception that basic reading instruction is introduced. Although the same format is continued, there is more structural activity and less free-time during which the three-year-olds play with toys. An interesting adaptation is the integration of typical American nursery rhymes, such as "Twinkle, twinkle, little star," as vehicles for moral and ethical lessons. The songs, of course, are translated into Yiddish and key words are changed to correspond with the intended theme. For instance, the last line of "Twinkle, twinkle," will be sung, "If you say Shema each day/ everything will be okay." The Shema is a fundamental prayer recited in the morning and evening. The same particular awareness of the relationship between the world of material objects and the prescribed way to behave in relation to those objects is stressed throughout the curriculum in the Kindergarten as well as in the Nursery School.

Women are employed as teachers at both the Kindergarten and Nursery levels. The children, the administration feels, are still young enough to warrant the attention and care of a mother figure. Also, it is felt that a man's ability as a Torah scholar should not be diverted to the tasks of teaching in the pre-school.

Every class has a teacher and an assistant, both addressed by the children as _Morah_ (teacher). Usually, the assistant is a younger girl, not yet married or engaged, who has just completed her own schooling and is in training to teach her own class.

The Bobover prefer that their teachers come from the community, or from other Hasidic groups. However, the demand for enrollment is so great that non-Hasidic women have also been hired. The basic requirements, though, ensure that even if a woman is not from a Hasidic background, her religious and cultural background is similar to that of the Bobover. She must be able to speak Hasidishe Yiddish, that is, Yiddish with the particular Hasidic inflection and pronounciation. She must be well-versed in Jewish law and Hasidic observance; she must be a strict observer of the laws herself.

All of the teachers have attended a girls' Yeshiva, usually a Beth Jacob school, and have also had a year's training at the Teachers Seminary Program conducted at Beth Jacob. The Bobover have only recently begun to expand their female educational facilities. The goal is to create an educational system for Hasidic girls which will obviate the necessity of sending them out from under direct community supervision to receive an education. But until such time as this institution comes to fruition, the women who teach in the Nursery and Kindergarten will continue to receive their training at non-Hasidic Yeshivas.

The women who teach in the pre-school classes are all enthusiastic about their work; they feel they are performing "in something worthwhile." Some, who have taught in the same capacity at other Yeshivas, express approval of the concept and curriculum that the Bobover have developed.

> In other Yeshivas [where I taught] there's nothing compared to this for children. There they were only concerned with Boom! getting the boy to Chayder and Gemorah. But here, there's a real interest in making a whole human being, not just a great head [for learning Torah]. Some people complain that this is too progressive and not Hasidishe enough. But what's not Hasidishe? I like teaching here because they do something with the children, not just let them sit until they're five years old.

The pre-school programs operate during the summer months as well. The curriculum is expanded to include more outdoor activities, such as daily outings to nearby parks, where children have a chance to participate in supervised games of tag, kickball, or play with an assortment of slides, swings, and monkeybars available at all New York City playgrounds. Swimming is an approved activity, not just for younger children, but for older students as well. And so, several times a week during the summer, the children are taken to a local pool, reserved exclusively for use by the Yeshiva, and given swimming instruction. The more conservative elements among Hasidic groups disapprove of such behavior. But the Bobover feel that in order to comply with their rigorous scholastic program, the students must be healthy in both body and mind.

Much of the substance of the child's nursery and kindergarten experience is contiguous with the home environment, although the presentation at home does not have the same structured perspective as the Yeshiva. From the time a child can speak, he is gently coaxed to attempt the prayers recited before and after meals, upon rising or before going to sleep. Older siblings, as well as parents, continuously encourage the young child to perform the simplest rituals, like covering one's eyes while reciting Shema.

The numerous holidays, each with its own particular observance and attendant objects, represent a major influence in the events at home. Children are always integrally involved in helping to prepare foods, arrange ceremonial objects, or assist in the ceremony itself on any given holiday. Major holidays, such as Purim, Passover, and Chanukah provide children with specific roles which, to the child, seem indispensible.[6] The lesser holidays, of which there are many, are occasions for simple lessons, explanations and stories at the dinner table or afterwards.

Hasidism has a strong oral tradition which is kept alive today through the transmission of legends and anecdotes from father to son. Quite often, a casual event or a religious occasion will prompt the retelling of a relevant tale from Hasidic folklore. Implicit in such recountings is the continuity of Hasidism, of which the child is an integral part. Tales about great Hasidic Masters of the past are peppered throughout with references to some recent comparable action performed by the Bobover Rov, or another contemporary Tzaddik (righteous man). Some stories are told with such regularity that kindergarten children, after their own fashion, will repeat them when prompted by a specific situation. As Jerome Mintz has shown, Hasidim from various courts and diverse national backgrounds all share a common wealth of these tales and anecdotes covering an inexhaustable variety of human experience.

From its inception, Hasidism has been characterized by the ecstatic nature and spontaneity of the songs and dances which accompany celebrations. The nigunim sung by Hasidim are songs of ecstasy composed by past and present Rebbes. Children learn the more traditional songs as a matter of course at home, where they are accompanied by all male relations. The Bobover Rov is a gifted composer of the nigunim, and naturally his Hasidim take delight in performing them and teaching them to their children. In 1974 a record was produced of Bobover Yeshiva <u>bochim</u> singing favorite nigunim. Since phonographs are not forbidden **objects** to orthodox Law, many Bobover households have collections of Hasidic nigunim performed by various courts, in addition to the Bobover recordings. Consequently, Hasidic children now learn the nigunim before even participating in group singing at the Rov's <u>tish</u>. The tish (literally table) is a weekly event in Hasidic communities where the males gather to receive symbolic morsels from the Rov's dinner. This feeding of the congregation is followed by a discourse on some subject in Torah, and singing and dancing. The use of the phonograph also allows the child to learn far more songs than he could by just listening and repeating those sung around the house. But, to many people, the recordings are a "poor imitation for the real thing," as one fourteen year old said. "It's so much more beautiful at the Rov's tish when everyone is singing and dancing. It's really something the heart can see, not like a record player, which is nice, but not the real thing." Nevertheless, the phonograph and the record provide children with a feeling for the nigunim and their contagious rhythms long before they are able to participate in the activity at the Rov's tish.

II

In Europe, education and economics were integrally related. Many families could not afford to indulge their children in anything more substantial than basic Chayder. Yeshiva instruction was reserved for students whose intellects merited patronage from a single benefactor, or a community fund, or sons of financially comfortable families. Girls were educated at home, where their education mainly consisted of learning basic female religious roles, such as lighting Sabbath candles, keeping kosher, caring for the children, and general housekeeping tasks. In some cases, students would shift from job to job, hoping to save enough money to allow themselves a few months free time each year to sit in the Yeshiva or Bes Hamedresh. The curriculum in European Yeshivas was flexible enough to allow such transience.

> In Europe, my father was what you'd call a freelancer...he'd do one thing or another. One time he found a shteibl with many unbound books. He made a deal to bind all the books in one week. He took the books home, put all his brothers to work, and made enough money to study for a few months. This was around the time he was Bar Mitzvah.

In America, such marginal or privileged education does not exist. For one thing, the law requires compulsory education until a child's sixteenth birthday, child labor being strictly prohibited. And also, the economic situation allowed a family to live, and even thrive, without demanding labor from every family member. Boys were free to fulfill the mitzvah of learning Torah.

At the time Hasidim began arriving in this country, New York had many established Orthodox Yeshivas which were scholastically acceptable by Hasidic standards. However, they also maintained behavioral attitudes which would facilitate assimilation into American society. Thus, the need for an educational system which would comply with existing governmental statutes without forsaking the cultural identity and solidarity of the Hasidic group brought into existence the American Hasidic Yeshiva: a synthesis of past and present. Structurally, it takes its example from the typical American public or private school. While subject matter has remained the same, teaching methods and presentation have undergone perceptible alteration.

A child's formal education commences with his attendance in the first grade. The grade system, like report cards, official tests and test scores, honor rolls, Nursery School and Kindergarten, is another innovative phenomenon in the Hasidic Yeshiva. Traditionally, there was Chayder, where basic reading and writing were taught; Yeshiva, where Torah and the commentaries were read and studied; and Bes Hamedresh, where advanced and endless learning was pursued.

The needs of the community in America, however, rendered the old system useless. Adapted to comply with an abundance of students, and with government regulations concerning the proper structure for educational curricula, the Chayder and Yeshiva have been compartmentalized into grades and classes. The structure, however, still maintains some of the flexibility of its European predecessor. Aside from the first and second grades, which are roughly equivalent to the Chayder, students are assigned to grades on the basis of ability, rather than age. Children who show uncommon ability in comprehension and discourse of Torah are invariably placed in classes among older, more advanced students. Similarly, a child whose abilities fall below the normal standard for his age will not be promoted in deference to a standardized system, which relies upon age uniformity for organization. Instead, he will be placed on a level which corresponds to his abilities. Unlike a similar secular situation, academic placement by ability, rather than age, does not result in either educational or social disruption for the child. This is due, in part, to the nature of the subject matter: Torah in its narrowest sense. The Pentateuch is basically finite. Every Sabbath, a different section of Torah is recited as part of the prayer service. When the last section is read, the holiday of <u>Simchas Torah</u> (rejoicing of the Torah) is celebrated, and the reading begins anew on the following Sabbath. Similarly, the educational curriculum, whose basis is Torah, is cyclical rather than lineal. What differentiates one grade from another is the depth of commentary on a particular *parsha* (weekly section), rather than the introduction of continuously new subject matter. The same topics appear year after year, from the first grade on. Only emphases and interpretations vary, and these according to teacher and individual student.

An administrator of the Yeshiva contends that the flexibility maintained by the educational facility is beneficial to the community as well as the individual student:

> A mind, any mind, must have stimulation. Too much is no good, too little is no good. Perhaps we have a boy who cannot keep up with what his Rabbi teaches. There is no shame. Torah was made for everyone. And since everyone is different, Torah is different. So if a boy can't understand on one level, he understands on another. The clever boy and the dull boy are the same then. One may lose interest because it's too easy, the other because it's too hard. If the mind is not kept interested, who knows where it will go, and where the body will follow. So we try to give each student what he will understand.

This idea is not peculiar to the Yeshiva, but is pervasive throughout the community. The high point of any week in a Hasidic community is the Rov's tish. In a community where status is accorded to the learned and the holy, the Rov stands alone. Yet, his weekly discourse invariably holds meaning for every man listening. Some of his teachings take the form of simple stories and parables, while others rely on obscure and esoteric tracts. The emphasis at each discourse in on raising the consciousness of all men, not just those intelligent enough to comprehend the abstract and esoteric.

Upon entering the first grade, the child assumes a new role, that of a Yeshiva bocher. He is given his own <u>S'forim</u> (books), an assigned seat, and for the first time he will be instructed by a male teacher. Although the distinction between Kindergarten and first grade is blurred somewhat by continued indulgence by parents and teachers, and the presence of some playtoys, like building blocks, the child's self-image as a serious student is clearly developing. At home, he will sit along with his father and older brothers and study the new words he has learned, or study the prayers he is expected to recite in class. If interrupted by a younger sibling, he will show annoyance, complaining, "I have to study!" Such seriousness at age five or six seems somewhat pretentious, but it is heartily encouraged by teachers, parents, relatives and friends.

The curriculum in the first grade is divided between material from the <u>Sidur</u> (prayer book) and holiday observance. The Sidur is actually used in conjunction with a basic primer. Since prayer is a central activity both for the individual and the community, it is imperative for children to be familiar with the prayer text and content as soon as possible. Reading exercises revolve around various sections of the Sidur. And reading exercises are never glossed over or taken lightly. In the course of a typical school day, reading exercises are conducted in the morning, before lunch, and in the afternoon before dismissal. Every child is expected to recite individually from the Sidur during the course of each reading session. Students are chosen at random, often in mid-sentence, and some are called upon several times in one lesson. And although admonition is gentle, the embarrassment of being caught day-dreaming during reading keeps even a five-year old's attention riveted to the book.

To minimize boredom and flagging attention, lessons are short and continuously interspersed with other learning activities. By the time a child has reached first grade he is familiar with dozens of songs, taken either from prayer services or other festivities. These, and new tunes, are used to relieve the tedium of reading. "For the young ones to sit and learn all day only dulls the mind," a teacher in the Chayder explained. "We try to make a balance between serious study and lighter things, like songs. If you give them a little, a little, a little, then they catch something--more than if you give them a lot at once." Very often a Rabbi will choose a prayer from the reading material, one which his students have performed well, and teach its melody in conjunction with the formal recital. In this way, a child learns to recite prayers passably well, and is able to participate to some extent in adult prayer services. At this age, a child has not yet acquired a full sense of what is being recited, but he is keenly aware of being a participant in group activity.

In the first grade, the holidays still provide the focus for daily lessons. Much of what is presented in the home and in the pre-school is reviewed. However, since learning to read is the key function of the curriculum, holiday texts, such as the Passover Hagadah or the Purim Megilla, serve as supplements to the daily prayers. Explanations and descriptions of various holidays do not vary from previous instruction, but the child's responsibility for observing the particular nuances each celebration demands is increased. On Passover, for instance, a Chayder bocher is expected to recite, by heart, the Four Questions before the gathered family. So, for two weeks before the event, Hagadah are distributed daily in class, and a constant round of repetitions, first of reading, then singing the text ensues. By the second week, the books are no longer used, and each child is expected, when called upon, to sing the Four Questions. A hesitant or faltering voice gives rise to shouted corrections from classmates. The text is also used, as before, to explain reasons and forms of observance. The presentation is all very straightforward and primarily concerned with developing basic skills upon which further study and prayer depend.

By the first grade, arts and crafts and free play activities of the Nursery and Kindergarten have been eliminated. Perhaps as a token to transition, the children are given a recess after lunch, during which snap blocks and wooden blocks are brought out for use. These objects, however, are treated more casually than the year before. Some children won't become involved with the blocks, prefering to sing that day's particular song, or other songs, rather than play with "baby things." By the second grade, there are no more building blocks, nor are they missed.

Instruction in reading and writing continues through the second grade, with material for lessons being drawn from the same basic sources. A major difference is the inclusion, for the first time, of Torah texts. For the most part, these are incorporated into the reading lessons. But invariably with each reading exercise comes an introductory lesson in the study of Torah.

At this point in a child's educational development he can read competently enough so that basic recital does not present much of a problem. Depending upon skill and the amount of practice a student puts in at home, the improvement over the previous year is noticeable. The Rabbis, in an attempt to retain precise pronounciation without hampering a student's reading rate, use Torah lessons to stress the importance of clarification. "If they read this fast at seven years old," one Rabbi exclaimed, "by ten, even we will have trouble understanding. And by thirteen, no one, not even the students, will understand a thing." The examples used by the Rabbis to make this point are simple by comparison, but startling to youngsters whose minds are untrained in Torah discourse. The usual method is to change one letter in a word, thus changing the word and, consequently, the meaning of the sentence. These simple lessons are quite effective, for afterwards reading rates slow down considerably.

Many lessons still revolve around the holidays. But since the second grade is an initiation point in the use of Chumesh, the explanations and technical descriptions are often more involved with specifics rather than generalities. As the child progresses further along in the Yeshiva, the generalities about the holidays and points of law disappear completely, and his mind is trained to deal with the minute and abstract logic that produced the tomes of commentaries he studies in conjunction with Torah.

Prayer also takes on another dimension. Previously, a child's experience with prayer was coincidental. At home specific prayers are taught and recited individually or in the company of brothers and father. In school the Sidur is used as a text. The traditional prayers recited before and after eating apply in school as well as at home. On the Sabbath and holidays some children accompany fathers to synagogue, and are expected to participate to the best of their abilities--which before second grade are minimal. However, an integral part of a child's enculturation concerns his conformity to synagogue behavior and ritual.

Hasidic prayer services are noted for their intensity and display of emotion. To an uninitiated observer such a service seems particularly disorganized. Men swaying and rocking in every conceivable direction, hands motioning expressively; even the volume and rapidity of the prayers themselves have no seeming unity of purpose. Such behavior, however spontaneous, is considered proper and expected. Hasidim believe that fervent prayer, whether spontaneously generated from within, or initially consciously adopted, will ultimately result in a more personal experience. Hence, children are expected to take their example for prayer behavior from their elders, despite the fact that they are not yet possessed by the same emotional spontaneity.

To nurture such responses, and to acquaint the child with the necessity of praying three times a day, in the morning, the afternoon, and the evening, congregational <u>davnen</u> (prayer) is introduced in the second grade. The exercise closely models the actual service in every way but length.

One student, chosen to lead the prayers, stands in front of the room trying to maintain a slim lead over his zealous congregation in the recital. At the beginning of the school year, the service consists of a brief selection of prayers from each service. As the students become more proficient, a new prayer is added every week until, by the end of the year, an entire service is covered in the same time it took to recite a few basic prayers. Occasionally, the Rabbi will request a certain prayer to be recited in addition to the usual ones. These requests are usually for specific Sabbath prayers, difficult to read without constant practice. Since boys, by this time, are expected to pray conscientiously on the Sabbath, fumbling and hesitation in class give witness to slack, irreligious behavior, which "you can believe doesn't happen twice."

Davnen together from this age on, a Rabbi points out, "makes the boys feel like comrades, more than just students together...if they davn together they get closer to God and closer to each other." Even though school begins at nine o'clock for the second graders, morning prayers are not held until an hour later, to insure that the entire "congregation" is present. The hour before is spent studying the section of Torah to be studied through the day. Evidently, the Rabbi feels it is important enough to have the entire class davn together, "If a boy comes late and misses some

Chumesh that is alright. We learn the same parsha over and over throughout the morning. So if he misses the first he'll get it the second time. But it's not good to miss davnen even once."

Specific teaching methods in the Yeshiva vary from Rabbi to Rabbi. But invariably, recitation and repetition, call and response, take overwhelming precedence over written exercises. In some appropriate situation, physical models or blackboard diagrams are used in conjunction with the primary text. For instance, the parsha which provides directions for the proper construction of the Mishkan, the holy ark which contained the original Mosaic tablets, is accompanied by a plastic and wooden model. Or the description in the Torah of a proper Menorah (ceremonial candelabrum) will prompt a diagram to be drawn, complete with labels. This method, however, is confined to a few lessons, scattered throughout the school year. And as a child advances through the Yeshiva, this limited innovation is dispensed with entirely.

The study of Torah is firmly based on an oral method, which takes a number of forms. A man may sit and learn by himself, chanting the primary text alone or in conjunction with the commentaries. Two men may Chazer (literally, to repeat), that is, study jointly, one rhythmically reading the primary text while the other interjects points of contention or clarification drawn from a particular commentary, which is printed alongside the primary material. Two men may also study conflicting or supportive commentary in this fashion. Torah study also includes pure lectures, where one man, usually an authority on a specific topic, will lecture to a class in the <u>Mesivta</u> (roughly equivalent to High School) or to the entire Bes Hamedresh, drawing his material from primary as well as secondary sources. The reading of Torah and commentaries is done according to specific rhythms and tones, which serve as an oral grammatical structure. The integration of these rhythms and tones with comprehension, and the ability to perform spontaneous feats of logic for which Talmudic scholars are historically noted, is the basis for the teaching methods used in the Yeshiva. The ability to think and respond quickly and precisely is developed through the call and response technique in the classroom. "Speaking is faster than writing. Thinking is faster than speaking. So a mind trained to think will make speaking and writing easier, too." This is the assumption which gives conviction to method.

From the first Torah lesson, students follow a course of study which leads them step by step to the advanced classes in the Bes Hamedresh. In the first and second grades where comprehension and reading skills exist on a rudimentary level, intonation and inflection are loosely observed. By the third and fourth grades where reading skills are improved, the Rabbis will often beat out the correct cadence, reading along with the class to set the correct tones. In the third grade, the commentaries are introduced to supplement the Chumesh. Morning classes concentrate on the primary text, usually the parsha that is to be read in synagogue that Sabbath. Afternoons are dedicated to a small section of <u>Rashi</u>, the classic eleventh century commentary written by Rabbi Shlomo Yitzhaki; commenting on the specifics of the morning lessons; or if the class is advanced and attentive, some Gemorah, a much more difficult exercise. Since there are precise rhythmic and tonal patterns for the commentaries as well as the Torah, the Rabbi will continue to read along with the class through the afternoon lessons. Very often, to set the example, he will read through the entire section slowly and precisely before allowing the class to attempt it.

The same subject matter is likely to be repeated through the school week, which commences on Sunday and ends on Friday at noon for the lower grades. For the first two days, the Rabbi will patiently proceed through the readings, refusing to accelerate despite the prodding of the brighter students. By midweek, however, the pace quickens, and students who cannot respond when called upon are ignored in favor of one

of the urgently waving hands. In some cases, a Rabbi will
allow a student an extra minute or two, or may even prompt
him somewhat with clues which take a logical step-by-step
towards the answer. But by Thursday, the last full day
of the school week, neither prompting nor hesitation are
tolerated; as a question is asked, an answer must be given.
In more advanced classes, students' answers will often be
turned upon themselves and require nimble shifting to avoid
the logical snares set by the Rabbi. But in the lower
grades, simple, straightforward answers usually suffice.
On occasion, a Rabbi will persist in grilling an extremely
gifted student beyond the student's abilities; by the same
token, he will give less intelligent students the simpler
questions to answer or the simpler phrases to read. Otherwise, "we would only be left with geniuses, of which there
are only a few in the entire Yeshiva, everyone else would
lose interest and become like a shoemaker or work in the
[diamond] Exchange by Bar Mitzvah."

    Although this method of teaching Torah is an extremely
effective way of imparting the subject matter while maintaining a high level of attention, it also proves exhausting.
From time to time, during a lull in afternoon classes, young
scholars' heads drop sleepily, only to be pulled upright by
a Rabbi's sharp voice. Many classrooms keep their windows
wide open, even during the coldest months, to combat fatigue.

The Rabbis are aware of the weariness brought on by such vigorous mental activity, but feel it builds character and resolution in a child if he "fights his physical urges to learn Torah." Fatigue is a problem of the afternoons; in the morning classes it is the opposite. In the mornings, when students and Rabbis are fresh, the energy generated by intensive repetition and response builds, and must be restrained lest it interfere with concentration. A student's slip while answering or reading touches off a flurry of wildly waving hands, moans, and bodies half raised from their seats. Such zeal is encouraged and even precipitated by the Rabbi, whose smile or corroborative nod to an answer is a valued reward. Punishment, on the other hand, is not meted out to those who hold back and refrain from the general din. There is, however, little tolerance for those students whose zeal is a mere facade, with no urgent answer to bolster it. And even in the third grade, where such behavior first appears, there is open derision of classmates who feign excitement to mask their ignorance.

Lunch periods, which last from forty minutes to one hour, are more of an excuse for releasing energy and restlessness from three to four hours of sitting and learning. Food is bolted down in a few minutes, in order to allow more time to run around on the street in front of the Yeshiva. The younger children, those under age thirteen, who have not adopted the customary long black bekesher and wide-brimmed hats, are allowed to play at tag or even throw a rubber ball among themselves. Older students who do not return immediately to their studies clear their heads by walking, in groups, up and down the block. During the lunch hour, 48th Street is barricaded to traffic and the children all remain in the immediate vicinity of the Yeshiva. Although the Bobover allow their younger children to play ball and games of tag during this period, some Rabbis do not condone such behavior and prefer their students walk with them to the Rov's house and back until recess has ended. Ball playing and other such frivolous activities are considered "un-Hasidishe" by certain conservative elements in the community. Their conviction is that if it is condoned, if only during lunch recess, it will affect a child's behavior, possibly tempting him to play ball at other times and engage in "other goyish activities." However, a more moderate view is taken by the administration, who realize that a Bobover child spends almost no time in the streets of Boro Park without adult supervision. In fact, children and adolescents spend very little time in the streets at all.

Testing in the Yeshiva is a weekly procedure. Tests consist of two parts: a written portion administered and graded by the teacher and sent to the Principal for scrutiny, and an oral part, conducted by the Principal himself. Both parts of this examination are taken directly from material covered in class throughout the week. Despite an impossibly crowded schedule, the Principal of the Yeshiva finds time to personally question every class each week. Time does not allow the oral testing of each child, but the possibility of being one of those chosen at random has the desired effect on student preparedness. An unsatisfactory performance on either part of the weekly exam results in a phone call to the pupil's home, thus generating enough concern or embarrassment to rectify the academic neglect.

Parents are kept abreast of their children's progress in school by periodic report cards and regularly scheduled "open school" weeks, both of which were introduced to the Yeshiva system in this country. Contact, however, between the Yeshiva staff and the child's home is not restricted to these two means. The level of familiarity in a small community is rather high, and parents do not feel inhibited about calling administrators or teachers to inquire about their child's particular problem. Teachers who are Bobover Hasidim see their pupils along with their parents in synagogue, or at any number of community functions, and expect to be consulted about a child's behavior and scholastic abilities. Those teachers who live in Boro Park but are not affiliated with the Bobover welcome inquiries from parents who stop them on the street or call their homes at night.

In the formative years of a child's development, his behavior is closely monitored and regulated by the home and Yeshiva environments. In later years, as he passes through adolescence to adulthood, the peer group will, to a great extent, replace the home and Yeshiva influences in dictating his behavioral prerogatives.

Footnotes - Chapter II

1. This figure was offered by Professor Lucjan Dobroszycki of the Yiddish Scientific Institute in New York City.

2. This figure was offered by several members of the Bobover Community.

3. The Hasidim refer to the spectrum of secular subjects, such as mathematics, science, history, geography, which compose the non-religious curriculum, as English studies.

4. The custom of letting a child's hair grow until his third birthday is based on a law which forbids the pruning of a fruit-bearing tree for the first three years of its life. God cares for the tree for these first three years, seeing that it grows correctly; Hasidim hope the same for their children.

5. The tapes consist of a selection of songs and melodies popular among the Bobover Hasidim. Some were composed by the Rov himself; others are the compositions of past Hasidic Masters. Many of the nigunim (songs) a child hears in the classroom are sung every Shabbos at the Rov's tish (table), at weddings, and other celebrations. An early familiarity with these songs enables a child to participate in their recital long before he is an adult member of the congregation.

6. At the Passover celebration, for instance, the youngest child present is required to ask four ritual questions of the service leader. This recital is listened to attentively by the gathered company. On Chanukah, the Festival of Lights, it is the child's duty to light the symbolic candles each of the eight nights.

CHAPTER III

The routines that develop after the first and second grades remain relatively constant through the seventh grade classes. Beginning with the fifth grade students are paired in the afternoon classes to chazer. The method favored by most Rabbis is to pair a "strong" student with a "weak" one. The Rabbi circulates from group to group observing, correcting, and interjecting his own thoughts. But he is just as likely to maintain a discreet distance, allowing the students independence of thought and action.

While observing a sixth grade class one afternoon, I noticed that one boy had his arm around his study partner's shoulder as his free hand moved along the page directing the reading. The Rabbi, seeing my interest, came over and explained:

> This is part of the spirit in this Yeshiva, and to have the boys chazer at a young age helps things. You know, lots of boys come here who aren't from Bobov, maybe they are Hasidishe, maybe just very Orthodox. In this Yeshiva there's real friendships built up, not competitions. The Rov's teachings stress good feelings and love between people. In hard times it holds people together and in good times it's that much nicer. But the bochim here all feel it's important to help each other. And lots of them who come here never leave. They become real comrades with

the Bobover boys, go into their homes, marry their sisters. We are here to encourage one another.

This principle is evident throughout the community, but particularly so within the Yeshiva environment.[1] Since the physical facilities are all gathered in one building, contact between children, adolescents, and adults is maximized. Children are exposed to 'ideal' behavior, as are adolescents and adults, merely by association. And in keeping with the Rov's example, aberrance of any sort merits immediate attention and correction. Older students and adults feel it is their responsibility to help the children maintain the correct perspective about Hasidus and Judaism. Conversely, the onus of such responsibility creates a certain self-awareness which, in turn, assures that the "examples'" behavior will remain exemplary.

As a boy approaches Bar Mitzvah his behavior and attitudes begin to change noticeably. In class there will be less commotion, and squirming to answer questions abates somewhat. Ball games and wild free-for-all tag matches do not occupy his interests during lunch recess. And occasionally several of the pre-Bar Mitzvah will be allowed to come to the Bes Hamedresh to study and pray an hour or two before they are expected to attend class.

The administration encourages these modifications by designating the eighth grade, where most boys are about to or have recently become Bar Mitzvah, as pre-Mesivta. In doing so, a new status and religious responsibility is given to these students. They are no longer considered part of the grade school: They are contemporaries (or nearly) of the Mesivta students whose lessons take the form of lectures, whose clothes are truly Hasidishe, and whose days, from 6:00 a.m. to 10:00 p.m., are spent in each others' company in the Bes Hamedresh or in one of the rooms on the top floor of the Yeshiva, learning Torah.

> A week before I became Bar Mitzvah I went to the Rov's house at 7:00 in the morning with my father. He helped me put on my <u>Tefillin</u> for the first time and we davned together. I went to school one hour early that day and learned by myself until my class came. Something like that you don't forget. The next week I stopped wearing 'baby' clothes and began dressing more Hasidishe. Not just to do it; I really felt that way.

This is usually a boy's first private audience with the Rov since his third birthday. On that first occasion whatever recognition resulted from the event was purely ritual. But a boy's Bar Mitzvah audience occurs at an age when the increasing self-awareness of adolescence profoundly influences subsequent behavior. Any personal contact with the Rov has major significance. It is, after all, visible recognition by the community of a boy's changing status.[2] And the psychological impact on the recipient of this attention is evident. Further encouragements come from the Yeshiva administration (noted above), from teachers, and, of course, from the home environment. The result of these actions is a coalescing of the peer group which, from Bar Mitzvah on, becomes a focal point for male activities. The emergence of peer group solidarity among the Bobover Yeshiva students appears rather suddenly, coinciding with the onset of puberty, and only abates somewhat, seven or eight years later, as marriage and family responsibilities assume priority.

As late as seventh grade student contact is limited to classrooms, and, perhaps, attendance at holiday and Sabbath services in the Synagogue.[3] Their dress, sport shirts, dark pants, colored yamulkas, identifies them with the "babies." And their behavior, although somewhat more restricted, is not seriously considered apart from that of the younger students. A year's difference represents a dramatic departure from childish attitudes and behavior, and heralds a new intensity in word, thought and action. Spurred on by social, historical, and biological forces, the Mesivta bochim must contend with energies which are channelled differently than in less regulated secular societies. Rather than restrict these energies, thereby creating ramifications which could possibly prove damaging to the individual, as well as the community, the peer group becomes the medium through which individual drives are directed towards, rather than away from, the Hasidic experience.

The new role a boy assumes is manifested in adoption of traditional Hasidic attire and fervent devotion to study and prayer. Initially the Mesivta students will leave home an hour or two earlier than usual to learn with friends before the morning prayer service, when they will either davn together as a group, or in the Bes Hamedresh along with the adults. As boys grow older, the time they arrive at the Yeshiva gets earlier and earlier. By the age of fifteen or sixteen the students are gathering at 6:00 a.m. After learning for two hours they will all go to Mikva, the ritual bath, to wash before prayers. After prayers and a communal breakfast in the Yeshiva lunchroom, they return to studies and lectures. In the evenings, after taking supper at home, most return to the Yeshiva to spend several more hours studying together.

Mesivta curriculum consists of daily sheerim (lectures) on Gemorah, Halakha (laws), and independent study periods in the Bes Hamedresh. The only remnant of the grade school structure is the presence of a teacher, but his role is more strictly defined.

> The main difference between babies and bochim is that the Rabbi [in the Mesivta] is not here to make you learn. The Rabbi comes in here to learn. If we want to learn with him, fine; if not that's fine too. He can talk to a class or to four walls. In the lower grades the Rabbi asks questions to keep you at your books. But the older you get the more you learn alone.

In the lower grades the Honor Roll was introduced as an incentive to learn. Such devices to convey public recognition are no longer necessary in the Mesivta. For the Yeshiva system, although insular, is inclusive, and word of mouth spreads quickly from the Yeshiva throughout the community. But in Mesivta and the higher realms of Torah scholarship sheer intellectual ability, which elicits praise in the lower grades, is not enough. "As a baby you just recite, but the bochim must <u>feel</u> for what they learn." Emotion, a key concept in Hasidic philosophy, is stressed in scholarship as well as prayer. The importance of emotional attachment is evident when observing a class of adolescents or young men learning Torah or Gemorah. Every student has his own style of expression: some rock and sway rhythmically, others beat upon the table or bench. The patterns are mainly posturings learned through frequent exposure to men studying at home or in the Bes Hamedresh. But what is expected of a Hasid is more than just posturing. For "who is a man fooling if he shuckles back and forth like a tzaddik, but thinks of business or some other thing? Only himself. To the outside he looks like a big tzaddik. But the outside, what does that mean? God knows. So who is fooled?" Mesivta bochim are the most vociferous exponents of this philosophy. Since their energies are wholly directed towards study and prayer they respond heatedly to those classmates whose intensity slackens, or whose practice lacks conviction. "There are guys here who look very religious and act very bright," complained one young man, "but they just sit taking up air and space." This attitude is spawned in the lower grades but is diluted to some extent by the indulgent atmosphere at home.[4] Beginning with adolescence, though, the influence of that environment subsides as less time is spent with the family. A boy who continues to spend more time at home than with his classmates is suspect. His behavior reflects adversely on his, and his family's status. Consequently, boys are encouraged to rise a little earlier in the morning, and come home a little later at night. Reinforcement, once found in the home, is now transferred to the peer group.

Despite the intensity found among adolescents and young men sincerity, not tyranny, dictates relationships within the group. In the Yeshiva the emphasis is as much upon effort as upon results. A student who has ability but squanders it, is castigated far more severely than a student who perseveres despite his intellectual limitations. Competition among students in such an environment is non-existent, it is incongruous.

Solidarity has been enhanced by the formation of a Bochim Minyan (students' congregation) on Shabbos. Normally the entire community prays together on the Sabbath,

The young men, however, anxious to maintain the high level of devotion and energy experienced throughout the week, conduct their own Shabbos services in the shteibl adjoining the Rebbe's house. The older men protested such a move, but the bochim petitioned the Rov who supported their position. The situation and its resolution, as recounted by an eighteen year old, accurately portrays the values and thinking of the adolescents in the Bobover community.

> It's nice here on Shabbos. Everybody is in Shul. Fathers work all week, so on Shabbos they want to get some joy and see their sons davn. But the guys here wanted their own minyan. Why? Well, on Shabbos it takes a long time by the laynen (Torah reading)... we'd rather spend the time davnen and having Torah discussions. Of course, the fathers weren't too happy with this...we have it in our heads to make Bobov even more frum (religious). Altogether there are over a hundred of us davnen in the shteibl. There is a strong feeling between us. The Rov supports us in this thing. He says the same thing went on in his father's time, so why shouldn't we have it too? I'm not saying we feel more strongly than our fathers, but they have other things on their minds, business affairs, family affairs. The bochim have just God and Torah, which is really the same. Torah is like the clothing of God.

Though such action may be misconstrued as adolescent rebellion it is actually in accord with Hasidic traditional ideals and recent Hasidic experience. Initially, adolescence appears to offer more freedom to a boy. The closed environment that exists between home and Yeshiva becomes flexible, seemingly to allow more mobility in expression and general movement. This, of course, is not the case, for there is no real choice in direction. Societal expectations and enculturation determine direction, and peer pressure defines limits and extremes. Until a boy is married and established as a family man he is not likely to be given a mandate for independence. Bobover society acknowledges adolescence as a period of growing conflicts and restless emotions; authoritarian restraint can often produce adverse reactions. So, rather than impose stricter controls from above, the Hasidic community encourages fraternal cooperation among peers. When questioned on the validity of such an approach, the Bobover refer to their adolescents during World War II.

> When the war came the whole Yeshiva was rounded up. These were mostly older boys over thirteen and healthy...so they were sent to work camps and not to the death chambers. Together they helped each other not just in a physical way, but in a spiritual way too. You know it's harder to be religious when you're alone and everything works against you. But with these boys it was different, they had each other as examples. If one was weak he would be held up by the stronger ones.

In Mesivta classes the peer group replaces parental supervision to a large degree. Although they have all received the same basic training at home and at the Yeshiva, individual preferences and interests are exhibited by each boy. A sense of correct behavior, Hasidishe behavior, takes precedence over individual deviations. Indulgence in contrary behavior is not tolerated by the group; the majority acts quickly to reprimand any member whose demeanor reflects negatively on his comrades.

Secular society offers a wider range of behavioral options through which excessive and confusing adolescent emotions may be expressed without producing anti-social behavior. Variety, though, can often lead to indecision and further frustration. Hasidism offers asceticism as an acceptable alternative which may be carried to extremes without being detrimental to societal goals and values. Asceticism has been an accepted phenomenon throughout Jewish history. The legends of great Hasidic masters of the past, told and retold to young children, are filled with examples of seclusion and corporeal denial.[5] Fasting, prescribed on several occasions throughout the year, is experienced at a young age. "It's a big thing for a nine year old to try to fast for a whole day on Yom Kippur. Even if he makes it only until lunch it's a good thing because he's trying it out."

Young children are encouraged to experiment peripherally with ascetic forms, but these are not stressed. Strong ascetic tendencies first appear during adolescence, when there is a more valid motivation for removing oneself from the world.

Although asceticism can be myriad in form, most bochim choose the acceptable alternatives founded in prayer and study. Leaving the community to study in another Yeshiva was a common practice in Europe. In Europe, such travel

was limited by cost and available transportation. Today
neither seems to present an obstacle, and many boys once
past their Bar Mitzvah take advantage of the opportunity,
although few see it as a vacation. Most who choose to leave
the community to attend Yeshivas in New Jersey, upstate New
York, London or Israel do so to limit their access to comfortable, familiar surroundings. "I am going next year to
London," stated one fourteen year old. "Why?" "Because
there you have less distraction from study. In London there
is nothing to do but study. It's a small Yeshiva, and they
watch you closely. You don't study...out!" The Yeshivas
in Wildwood, New Jersey and Monsey, New York, offer the same
advantages: isolation and strict supervision.[6]

There are those students who, rather than change environments, impose rigorous study habits upon themselves.
Many nights they will fall asleep over their books in the
Bes Hamedresh, awake abruptly and begin reading again with
enforced vigor and concentration. They see travelling to
another Yeshiva as the easy way out. "How much harder it is
to concentrate on Torah and God when there are distractions
than when there are none."

Beginning with pre-Mesivta the grade structure maintained by the Yeshiva is discontinued. A student's level
of study no longer has a numerical association such as
first, second, and third grade, but a Rabbinical and textual

reference. When asked what their status is in school, students will reply with the name of the text and the name of the Rabbi who delivers the daily lectures. A Rabbi who delivers the daily sheer is referred to as a <u>Rosh Yeshiva</u> (head of the Yeshiva), a title given out of respect since, in reality, none of these lecturers are truly the Rosh Yeshiva.[7]

Attainment of Mesivta status allows a boy access to the Bes Hamedresh. Attendance at the sheerim, however, is mandatory for the first three or four years in Mesivta. And since the sheerim are delivered from 9:00 in the morning until 3:00 in the afternoon, the actual time a Mesivta student spends in Bes Hamedresh is limited to a few hours in the early morning and the late afternoons and evenings. At these times the bochim mingle freely, for the first time, as contemporaries with the adults.

By the third or fourth year of Mesivta some students choose to skip one or two sheerim a week to spend more time in the Bes Hamedresh. Such behavior is tolerated, but not encouraged, if a student shows ability and a real desire to learn. Although attendance is not checked, it is carefully noted by the <u>Mashgiach</u>, the director of the Bes Hamedresh, who is quick to remind younger students of the sheerim they are required to attend. Those few students who display unusual ability are allowed to forego more than an occasional sheer in order to chazer with an older scholar in the Bes Hamedresh.

Educational transitions from the ages of approximately seventeen or eighteen onwards are based on personal motivation, rather than pre-determined goals or requirements. Since the logic of graduation does not apply to Torah studies in Hasidic Yeshivas, the time when a student stops attending sheerim to sit in the Bes Hamedresh on a full time basis is left to individual preference. Usually an older student will not forsake the sheerim altogether, but attend only those which hold some special interest for him. Special sheerim are given in the Bes Hamedresh several times a week by noted authorities on particular points of law or commentary. These are held in the rear of the Bes Hamedresh, and are attended by whoever is present plus any interested community member.

Attire, mentioned above as one of three elements which constitutes identity, undergoes the several modifications during Mesivta which bring it into full conformity with Bobover tastes and Hasidic prescriptions. Initially a student entering the pre-Mesivta exchanges his sweaters and colored shirts for a dark suit and a white shirt. He also begins wearing a soft, small brimmed black hat in addition to his yarmulka. By the second or third year of Mesivta individual preference determines fashion. Some students prefer to maintain a more modern image and continue wearing small brimmed hats, and plain dark suits. Others adopt the more traditional Ibitseer, or long coat (this is not to be confused with an overcoat, the Ibitseer replaces the short, tailored suit jacket) and a hat with a wider brim and higher crown referred to as a <u>Samat Kepelish</u>, a hat made from beaver fur or velvet. On Shabbos and holidays most Mesivta bochim, even those who wear more modern suits during the week, adopt the traditional bekesher, a long silk coat with pockets in the rear.

The style of dress a boy ultimately adopts usually results from three conditions: 1) family status in the community, 2) personal religious and cultural sentiments, 3) pressure to conform. As mentioned above, status in the community is based on learning and piety. At its inception Hasidism was based on emotion, not intellect. As it evolved, though, and Hasidim began emerging as scholars as well as saints, the two forces attained the compatibility that modern Hasidim exhibits today: that is, scholarship and spirituality go hand in hand.[8] In much the same way Hasidic dress, which at first reflected a period in the history of East European Jewry, lingered to become synonymous with the philosophies and behavior of one group from that period. As the particular clothing became part of a Hasidic identity it gained additional significance. For if Hasidism is a life in which every act, every thought is dedicated to God and Torah, even a man's clothing must serve more than ornamental and functional purpose: clothing, like behavior, becomes ritual. So among Hasidim, the more learned and pious a man is, the more Hasidishe his clothing will be. Therefore boys from highly regarded families are expected to adopt the most traditional garments their age permits. This does not imply that the sons of families whose status, as regards religious behavior, is considerably lower cannot dress just as Hasidishe. "There are boys here," commented a Rabbi, "who look like the sons of big Rabbomim, but whose fathers dress very modern, some without beards even. These boys dress like this because they have a strong feeling for being religious and Hasidishe." But as with prayer behavior, conformity without conviction results in condemnation. Among the Bobover pressure to conform concerning appropriate attire is moderated by a tolerance for a wide range of individual preference and the desire to encourage rather than coerce. There are certain standards which must be met, but beyond these what is acceptable is determined by the individual.

> Here [in the United States] nobody cares how you dress, you can go anywhere, do anything. There is a joke in the Yeshiva that someday it will be the style for everybody to wear shtreiml and bekesher...then it will look like all the Hasidim are waiting on line at the movies and working on Shabbos....I call

> my clothing a personal weapon because if I
> am tempted to do something which by law is
> not right one look at myself, my hat, my
> coat, my tstitsis reminds me who I am.
> Nobody is there to see except me, and believe me that's enough!

In the United States where diversity of fashion and personal preference for attire does not hamper social or economic mobility this concept of dress as a "personal weapon against sin and temptation" has become a familiar refrain among the Bobover in justifying their adherence to traditional garments.

This attitude has evolved from the reaction that occurred among the adherents to traditional Judaism in Eastern Europe to the demands of the Enlightenment and a more modern world in the latter part of the nineteenth century. The reaction took the form of a retreat into the past. Independent and innovative interpretation of the Judaic law all but ceased; social deviation became the equivalent of religious heresy. "Sins of immorality and venality were outranked by sins of modernity which became identified with atheism and even apostasy. Cutting one's earlocks, wearing a coat shorter than the traditional style, reading 'modern" books--these were the most pernicious sins of all."[9]

In Poland and Galicia, where the Enlightenment never gained the widespread acceptance it enjoyed in Western Europe, increasingly rigid governmental proscriptions helped stifle assimilative tendencies as well. Although in 1873, Galician Jews were the first among East European Jews to be granted the right to vote, they were still subjected to legislation which severely limited their economic opportunities.[10] In 1909, a government-sanctioned boycott of all Jewish merchants and merchandise was initiated in Galicia.[11] Poland enacted laws in the 1920's and 1930's regulating occupation as well as locality of habitation.[12] Some resistance, such as the general strike by Polish Jews in 1936-37, was inaugurated.[13] But the futility of an all-but-disenfranchised minority was painfully evident.

Among the Bobover today the reactionary attitudes of the nineteenth and early twentieth centuries have softened somewhat. Certain strictures, such as the ban on "modern" literature still remain in effect. But as regards dress, divergence from a rigid norm, while not openly embraced by the more conservative elements, is allowed to exist without drawing open hostility or negative sanctions.

Footnotes - Chapter III

1. Hasidim believe that the world God created will last for six thousand years. The first two thousand years were made for Torah, that is, when God gave the Jews the Torah. The second two thousand years were for Avodah, working, devoting ones life to God. The last two thousand years, which we are in now, is for Gimilas Hasidim--good deeds between one man and another. The Bobover Rov stresses this concept in his teachings. He sets an example by his actions which he expects his Hasidim to follow.

2. In addition to the Bar Mitzvah audience a boy is called upon on Shabbos after the reading of the Torah to deliver a small drusha, a discourse on some point of Torah or commentary. Traditionally this first drusha is supposed to exhibit a student's scholastic and spiritual progress. But in recent years, with the increase in the number of Bar Mitzvah, a bocher's first drusha has become a formality. Far more significant is the audience with the Rov.

3. Because of the school schedule and the restricted mobility of younger students little fraternizing occurs outside the Yeshiva environment. Some students do not even get to see their classmates on Shabbos because they either live too far from the Bobover Yeshiva or their families attend a different Synagogue

4. "When I was a kid," a Mesivta student explained, "it was easy to get away with things, not that I did anything really wrong. But sometimes, you know how it is with kids, you don't feel like sitting and learning something if it's too hard, even if it's good for you to know. My father after a few times caught onto these little tricks, but my mother was always on my side. And most of the time, she would have me lay down with some tea or something. 'Study?' she'd say, 'There will always be books. But how many eyes do you have?'"

5. A popular story, which I heard on several occasions while observing classes, relates how a young Rabbi

locked himself in a room the day after his marriage and refused conversation or food for three years. "And," the teacher related, "after three years he came out and he was a Rebbe."

6. The high standards of the Bobover Yeshiva in London have been achieved largely through the efforts of one man, a relative of the Rov, who [it is rumored] calls the Rov every week to report on the progress of all the students and of the community in general. Several years ago a group of Mesivta students went to learn at the London Yeshiva for six months. The austerity and energy of their common experience forged a group identity which, to this day, remains intact and synonymous throughout the community with serious scholarship and exemplary Hasidic behavior. They are known as "Londoners," a term which has become generalized to include all Mesivta bochim who embrace the same ideals. The original "Londoners," aware of their prestige, maintained a clannish relationship which initially alienated some of their peers. In time, however, the attitudes which fostered this superior stance softened and were replaced by pride and the desire to attain similar status throughout the group.

7. A Rosh Yeshiva does exist. He sits in the Bes Hamedresh to mediate in the event of conflicts between students and teachers concerning textual interpretation.

8. Lucy S. Dawidowicz, The Golden Tradition (Beacon Press, Boston, 1966), p. 15.

9. Dawidowicz, p. 74.

10. Bernard Weinryb, The Jews of Poland (Philadelphia Press, Philadelphia, 1973), p. 212.

11. Dawidowicz, p. 74.

12. Weinryb, p. 213.

13. Dawidowicz, p. 80.

CHAPTER IV

When the Bobover first arrived in this country, and perhaps for a decade afterwards, many young men were being matched and married before their nineteenth birthdays. There were two basic reasons for this. First, according to some of the young men who became <u>chusanim</u> (literally, grooms. The term applies from the time a man contracts an engagement to one year after the marriage.) during that time, after so many years of uncertainty and suffering, the older generation had a strong desire to see "<u>naches</u> (happiness) from grandchildren." Others insist is was necessary to build up the strength of the community, although "my parents didn't put it that way, I could see they still felt unsure here and were afraid the older I'd get the more I'd see and maybe, who was to know, want an American wife." For most of these young husbands marriage meant an end to fulltime studies. Those whose fathers or fathers-in-law were wealthy enough to support an additional household remained in the Bes Hamedresh; the majority went to work and studied on the Sabbath or in their spare time.

In recent years the average age for a chusan has increased to twenty and, in some cases, twenty-one. Since marital arrangements are parental responsibilities, and frequent social contact between males and females before marriage is strictly forbidden, boys now have an additional two to three years of uninterrupted study from the time their official association with the Mesivta curriculum terminates. These years are spent almost entirely in the Bes Hamedresh, reading and learning.

> The two years before I became a chusan were something special. I would get up in the morning, go to Bes Medresh, learn all day, no pressure of tests or Rabbis. At night the same thing. I didn't worry for anything, a wife, a job, what to do with myself. Just learning Gemorah, that's all I'd do.

At an age when adolescents in other communities are beginning to experience the pressures brought about by college acceptance and achievements, career demands, or marital obligations, Hasidic youths are indulged in what, for them, can only be defined as an ideal situation. Since education in Hasidic society is not identified with career preparation or economic incentives, motivation to learn is dictated by values which result in a much lower level of anxiety.

The Bobover educational system is designed to maintain community solidarity, without which Hasidism in this country cannot function. The values attached to wealth and recognition in a competitive environment are minimized both at home and in the Yeshiva while cooperation and the importance of a close knit group dedicated to a single religious ideal are constantly reinforced. Financial security, to be sure, is regarded as necessary to obtain the optimum living situation, but it is a means to an end rather than an end in itself.

Among Hasidim a career is not regarded as an area in which one achieves fulfillment and identity. These things are found in Torah study and community participation. "To make a living is important," said one young man, "to love your work is not." Since all adults in the community manage to find some type of work at jobs which do not impose restrictions on religious observance and participation in community affairs, the adolescent population does not concern itself with the problems of future employment. In fact the question of acquiring a job does not arise until a boy has become a chusan.

Transcribed below is a statement taken from a young man who became a chusan in December 1974 on the events which led up to his engagement. Although each situation naturally has its own peculiarities, the sequence of events related here follows the typical procedure among the Bobover.

> I never said anything, you know, about becoming a chusan. As a matter of fact, whenever the subject came up I would get pretty touchy. Like my mother would say, "do you want us to see a shadchen (matchmaker)?" I would get real defensive and say things like, "I don't care" or "I don't want to think about such things, do what you want." And really we're not supposed to think about such things. But some-

times you can't help it. This friend gets married, that friend gets married...sooner or later it's your turn...it's hard to keep it out of your mind. I just went about my business, trying to keep my mind on learning. Sometimes a father wants to marry his daughter to a real <u>talmud chucham</u>, he'll come to the Mashgiach and ask who's available. But my shadchen was from the [diamond] Exchange. Not a big shadchen who has dozens of matches, like a wholesaler, just a guy who does it as a sideline. He suggested this match with, of course, a religious girl with a good education, and my father was agreeable. I guess her father was agreeable too. The phone calls went back and forth arranging times and dates, the whole thing. I didn't want to know from it. But, of course, it was in the air, and that's when daydreaming really starts. So a meeting was arranged, and I wore, of course, my best Ibitseer, but with a more modern hat than I usually wear, to test the climate you could say, and we went to my <u>colla</u>'s house. Everything was very polite, I was on my best behavior: manners like I never had before, opening doors, little smiles, everything. We all sat around talking about this and that, and then the parents went into the next room leaving us alone to talk. Sometimes this will happen once before people make up their minds, sometimes two, even three times. More than three times, forget it! Things are never going to work out. So we talked. I was all set to make small talk, "what do you do? How's the weather?" just to start things. But my colla right away wanted to see if I was sharp or one of those guys who knows nothing. She starts off, and in English! A lot of girls today have had better educations in secular subjects than the boys, and they want to be able to talk about something other than the weather. I could see right away what was what. She asked me something in current events, you know what did I think about such and such...one thing went to another, we talked for over an hour. The parents figured it was enough for one time so they came back in. My colla and I discussed it afterwards, and we

knew it was alright after the first time...
so did the parents...nobody said anything.
I made like it was no big deal, we didn't
even discuss it too much at home. Even my
brothers didn't know.

So we had a second meeting. This time I
wore a more conservative hat, but a shorter
coat. This time we talked a little longer;
I think I did most of the talking. By then
we were really sure, but it waited for the
third time. My parents said what do you think,
her parents said the same, we agreed it was a
good match. I picked up a <u>gartl</u> (a cloth
belt tied around the waist during prayer) to
show I had given my word, blessings were
said, and we sat down to eat (among Hasidim
the custom is to forego eating at any meeting
between parents until an agreement has been
reached. The tradition follows the behavior
of Jacob who, when going to contract the
marriages of his daughters, insisted on stating his intentions before partaking in
refreshments).

The next week I went to see the Rov with a
kvitl to discuss my engagement. He gave me
his blessings. The next week we had <u>t'noyim</u>
to make everything formal. The t'noyim was
written up by the Rov's oldest son, I said a
few words, we sang some nigunim, drank <u>l'chaim</u>,
you know, celebrated.

I don't see my colla until the wedding; we
talk on the phone once or twice a week. By
the very religious families even this is not
done. I saw her walking in the street once,
with her mother, and I stopped to be polite,
but for a minute only. I try to keep my mind
on learning...but now I have to think about
what kind of work I can get too. So really
for the next few months concentrating on just
one thing is hard.

For a Hasidic youth on the threshold of marriage, the
range of employment possibilities is dictated by cultural
and educational limitations. Besides a Yeshiva education,
supplemented by a bare minimum of non-religious instruction,
the average Bobover adolescent has little to offer by

way of training or specific preparation required for most white collar jobs or specialist trades. Nor is he likely to apply for jobs which necessitate involvement in irreligious activities, such as the handling of non-kosher products, or close contact with women. The primary concern, however, when seeking employment is whether or not earning a living will interfere with religious observance on a personal or communal basis. For in addition to holidays such as Rosh Hashonah (New Year) and Yom Kippur (The Day of Atonement), which are observed by all Jews regardless of congregational affiliation, Hasidim require additional work-free days to celebrate minor, as well as major, holidays. Also, during the winter months when sunset, and hence Sabbath observance, occurs before 5:00 p.m., Fridays must, by necessity, become half days. Although Sunday is considered a weekday, and thus a work day by Hasidim, most non-Hasidic-owned businesses are closed.

Acquisition of wealth, or attaining a secure financial position, is not at all contrary to Hasidic values, as long as the religious behavior of the individual or his family is unaffected.[1] By relaxing certain regulations and restrictions Hasidim could avail themselves of a wider range of economic opportunities. Clearly, such actions are not even considered by the young men seeking jobs today. They are content to exist within the employment patterns established

by their elders in this country rather than compromise
their beliefs. On February 21st 1972 C.B.S. news presented,
as part of a news documentary, a report entitled "New York's
Poor Jews." An interview with a Hasidic family whose combined income was sufficiently low to qualify for the Government Food Stamp program, poignantly illustrated the prerogatives that exist in Hasidic communities. The family consisted of a father, who worked in the diamond exchange, his
wife, a part-time secretary, who supplemented her income by
babysitting for non-Hasidic working mothers in the community, and six children ranging in age from five to twelve.
The father explained that if he chose to ignore certain
religious practices he could get a better job, but "that
would mean working in the winter on Shabbos." The largest
expense, he asserted, was sending all six children to Yeshiva,
but this, too, was necessity. The family managed, even though
they had to forego many luxuries. There was no question
about priorities: "Bread you must have, without bread you
can't live. But if it's necessary rather than give up our
religion, we'll do without butter."

Employment opportunities for Hasidim fall into three
general categories: (1) self-employment, (2) community
employment, (3) outside employment. Self-employment is
limited to a variety of wholesale or retail businesses. For

the most part the retail businesses, if they deal in food and produce, will cater exclusively to a Hasidic and Orthodox clientele; they will seldom exist outside the community. Retail shops dealing in dry goods, such as clothing, materials, jewelry, and general merchandise may have a non-Jewish clientele as well, and thus may exist outside the community. Tailors specializing in Hasidic clothing may or may not be self-employed, depending on skill, capital, and available clientele. There are a few service businesses owned and operated by Hasidim such as plumbing and carpentry. But since these skills require previous training, the probability of young men fresh from Bes Hamedresh setting up their own plumbing service is highly unlikely. In most cases, a young man whose father owns a business will join him upon marriage or terminating full time studies, if the business can support two "self-employed" men.

On a wholesale level again, the same divisions apply as in retailing. Food distributors deal solely in Kosher products, the only difference being that their distribution may include non-Jewish-owned stores with a Jewish clientele. Importers deal in a wide variety of merchandise, from pearls and furs to plastics and papers. Again, a son will enter into a business and be considered self-employed only if the business is capable of supporting another family.

A small percentage of Hasidim own catering halls which

are patronized by community members and non-Hasidic Orthodox Jews. Some own nursing homes and manufacturing operations of various sizes.

    A questionnaire distributed among 200 Yeshiva and Mesivta students requested informants to list in order of preference desirable areas of employment.[2] Community employment in one form or another appeared on nearly three-quarters of all questionnaires returned. Among young students, the desire to become a "house bocher by the Rebbe," a student supported by the Rov himself, not only reflected the inherent status attached to such a position, but also displayed a general lack of information or motivation concerning future employment. This response predominated, to the nearly complete exclusion of other possibilities. Mesivta responses predictably displayed an increased awareness of job options outside the community. Again, as with the younger students, desire to work in the community ran close to seventy-five percent. But Mesivta students, unlike their younger comrades, had more definite ideas about the roles they wished to assume. Teaching in the Yeshiva and "working for the Rebbe"[3] were preferred occupations; the response that occured most frequently and always in "the most desirable" category, was <u>Kolel</u>.

    Kolel is a special division of the educational system which is attended by young married men only. It is elitist in the sense that while one attends Kolel on a full-time basis, he is not expected to hold any sort of employment. His "job" is to learn. In some cases, the new household is supported by either one or both sets of parents; in other cases, the wife will work for a year or two to allow the husband an additional few years to immerse himself in Torah and Gemorah before he assumes financial responsibility for the family. If a wife's salary is not sufficient to support a household, additional funds will be supplied by a Kolel fund established by the community for that purpose. In some instances, if a young man displays uncommon ability and desire to continue his studies in Kolel, the expense for supporting his family while he learns will be shouldered entirely by the community. Kolel funds are derived from contributions given for that specific purpose, and <u>Tziduka</u> (charity) given by community members in general, to the Yeshiva, the Bes Hamedresh or the Rebbe himself.

While the opportunity to attend Kolel is available to all, the economic situation shared by most young married couples necessitates an end to full-time studies. Bobover families have an average of five children, all of whom must be clothed, fed, and Yeshiva-educated. This factor, coupled with the limited economic range of the average Hasid, leaves a young married man little choice between Kolel and employment. Securing a teaching position in the Bobover Yeshiva or another sympathetic Hasidic Yeshiva is almost as desirable as Kolel. Although the responsibilities of teaching detract from time that could be spent learning, the 3 o'clock dismissal time still leaves several additional hours each day to sit in the Bes Hamedresh.[4]

Since there are only a limited number of jobs available within the community structure, and not every man can be self-employed, the majority of the Bobover seek employment in other areas.[5] The diamond exchange and the garment industry have been two areas in which considerable numbers of Hasidim are employed. Hasidim can be found on every level of the diamond trade, from importing to cutting and polishing. Initially, this was one of the few areas which offered the Hasid, with his limited training and strict religious prescriptions, a chance to earn something more than a minimum wage without compromising his principle beliefs and values. It is impossible to estimate how many Hasidim are engaged in the diamond industry; the Exchange, located off Fifth Avenue between 46th and 49th Streets in Manhattan, is filled with evidence of their presence. Aside from the Hasidim themselves, scurrying between stores and offices, each one with a small black sample case, there are several restaurants which serve only *glatt kosher*, food.[6] At five o'clock, long yellow buses with congregational names printed on their sides block traffic while waiting to carry their passengers to Crown Heights, Williamsburg, Boro Park, or

Spring Valley.[7] The Hasidic influence is so pervasive that by three o'clock on Friday afternoons, the normally hectic streets and stores are noticeably subdued; and on Saturdays, except for pedestrians, they are nearly empty.

In recent years though, young men in Hasidic communities have been seeking alternatives to working on the Exchange. "Sure, diamonds are a good thing, when everybody has money to spend there's lots of money to be made. But when times are hard, not so many people are rushing to buy diamonds and luxury things. Then we really feel it here. Big givers give less, and tziduka from small guys...forget it! It takes a week's commission just to feed the family." For this reason, Hasidic youth have branched out into other fields, taking instruction in bookkeeping and accounting, attending training programs in computer programming and basic electronics.[8]

As with any other major decision, Hasidim will seek the counsel of their Rebbe before committing themselves to a particular job. If the job is in a field such as diamonds, where social and religious sanctions have been previously established, seeking the Rebbe's advice is done more from respect and to receive his blessings than for actual consultation. However, if a young man has an opportunity to seek employment in an untraditional field, an audience with the Rebbe is imperative and significant in influencing the young man's decision. Several years ago, a young man with an unusual talent for lettering and design was offered a job, by an Orthodox but non-Hasidic Jew, as a commercial artist. The prospective employer had seen signs and illustrations the young man had produced for special occasions in the synagogue, for weddings, and for circulars distributed by the Yeshiva. On the basis of these projects, he was prepared to send the young man to school to be trained as a commercial artist and provide him with a high-paying job upon completion of the course. The confused young man sought the Rov's counsel. The Rov sympathized with the young man's desire to earn a good living and participate in something he enjoyed doing. Still, he cautioned against accepting either the schooling or the job. He suggested that the young man continue to employ his talents to assist the community, and seek employment which would not contradict his life-style or beliefs. The young man accepted the advice. He now works at a job which provides him with an adequate income to live in the Bobover community, and continues to direct the production of posters and signs for community functions, and leads, he says, "a good life."

> "A good life?" A young Hasid observed amidst the music and singing at a friend's wedding. "I'll tell you. Me and this chusan we'll never be millionaires. But with G-d's help, we'll make out. Who needs such a thing as a million dollars. Sure it's nice. But that I earn a living and can be here in Bobov that's more important. A year ago I

was a chusan. Now I'm a father. I have a job. I don't have to worry what's going to be. I walk in the street, I know everybody. I have somewhere to davn. At night I want to learn I go sit in Bes Medresh for a few hours. There's always somebody there. In three years my son will start in school, I don't have to worry that he has to go an hour by bus to a good school or that he should be with strangers or people who are not so religious. In Europe I don't think they had it so good. If you lived in Bobov or another big place with lots of Hasidim, maybe. But the Jew who lived in the shtetl or even a smaller place? To see the Rebbe meant some trip. Or school? If you were rich, if you were smart, if you lived near a school. How many parents could afford to send their sons to Yeshiva? Here some people say things could be better. Maybe. Meshiach (Messiah) could come. But for me it's enough. Look, see how many people are here at this chassanah (wedding). Look how many children. Every year they have to make plans to make bigger the Yeshiva or Bnos Zion. Why? Because nobody moves to Long Island or California. They all want to stay here by the Rebbe, by the Yeshiva, by the family, the friends. G-d's will, things will only get better. Of course, we pray for Meshiach, but until he comes I'll be happy to see that me and my family can live a Hasidishe life, a religious life. I can't think of anything better.

Footnotes - Chapter IV

1. Wealth can lead to even greater status if used for the community's benefit. Tziduka, charity, is a major mitzvah among Hasidim; naturally, any man who gives generously and often will be highly regarded in the community. Since all giving is made public through the gossip network, generous men are known throughout the community. Even the younger Yeshiva students will refer to elders as "big givers."

2. Yeshiva and Mesivta rolls are split nearly down the middle between Bobover and non-Bobover students. Many boys who come to study at the Yeshiva eventually stay in the community and consider themselves Hasidim of the Bobover Rov. Since I was interested in determining job preferences among Bobover Hasidim, statements are based on 113 questionnaires returned by Bobover students ranging in age from 9 to 18 years old.

3. The term "working for the Rebbe" is generally used to cover a wide range of services from acting as the Rebbe's secretary to representing him at various functions.

4. Working as the bus driver for the Yeshiva also allows a man extra hours in the day to study. Conversely, working in the administrative offices demands more time than a 9-5 job does. The opportunity to work for the community more than compensates for this inconvenience.

5. Solomon Poll lists a variety of occupations generated by the existence of the Hasidic community. These jobs vary from marriage broker to ritual slaughterer; although the variety exists the actual positions are limited in number.

6. The word glatt means smooth and refers to the condition of the animal's lungs upon being slaughtered. If there are lesions or damage to the lungs the meat of the animal cannot be pronounced strictly kosher in accordance with the Law.

7. Rather than ride the subways and be faced with the prospect of coming in close contact with women, which is unavoidable during the notorious New York City rush hour, many Hasidim prefer to travel to and from work in the Congregational school bus. Some buses are equipped to allow their passengers to observe morning and evening prayer services while commuting between one location and another.

8. Some corporations, such as RCA Electronics, have instituted training programs which result in employment complementing Hasidic religious observance. The correspondence course has also gained acceptance among Hasidim who shun most secular institutions. In this way studies can be done in spare time at home, without compromising moral or cultural standards.

APPENDIX I

In order to qualify for municipal, state, and federal financial assistance, Hasidic Yeshivas are required by the laws governing such programs to include secular education as part of the standard curriculum through the twelfth grade level. According to the Bobover Yeshiva administration, government subsidies, in the form of food, books and other educational materials, count for approximately 20% of the Yeshiva budget. For this reason alone, inclusion of an "English" department is desirable. Like any other social group, the Hasidic community consists of individuals who, while embracing a common set of values and beliefs, represent a diverse range of tastes, opinions, and behavioral preferences. For some, even minimal contact with secular elements is anathema; for others, the desire and necessity to participate to some extent in non-Hasidic activities can be realized without forsaking their Hasidic identity. However, the decision to supplement the centuries-old traditional educational curriculum in Orthodox institutions with modern studies has produced major conflicts within the Hasidic community.

The concept of "modern" studies itself is quite innovative and therefore suspect. Hasidim's reactionary nature developed in response to the pressures of secularization movements which threatened traditional East European Jewry from the eighteenth century onward. As a result, the preservation of past institutions became essential to Hasidic existence. The Yeshivas of Europe fought vigorously and successfully to exclude the slightest taint of secular education from their curriculum. In Russia and Poland, the governments, in an attempt to forcibly assimilate the Jews into majority culture, established State Yeshivas. Called "Crown Schools," these institutions offered an "enlightened" program of religious studies and "modern" studies.[1] The theory behind the formation of these schools was that Jews remained apart from the general society because of ignorance and superstition fostered by their archaic educational activities.[2] If offered the chance to break with superstition and receive "proper" rational educations, Jews would embrace the ideals and values of proper Christian society. To ensure enrollment, the government enforced a student quota from the Jewish population, which responded by volunteering marginal students, orphans, and the extremely poor. The best students remained in traditional Yeshivas.[3]

In the United States, no such direct coercion exists. Among the various groups which comprise the total Hasidic population, a handful offer more than token secular instruction. For the small shteiblich with Yeshiva rolls of no more than thirty or forty students, the inducement of Federal assistance is irrelevant; community contributions are sufficient to maintain a facility of that limited size. But to a Yeshiva of five hundred or one thousand students, community support alone cannot cover operational expenses; government resources are a necessity. Once the reality of secular education has been introduced in a Yeshiva, the extent to which it will become a factor in the lives of the children depends upon the attitudes and cooperation of community leaders and members. Even though a religious man such as the Rov may favor some secular education, he will refrain from speaking out about it in public too often, lest some people think he is becoming too liberal.

Among some groups, such as the Satmar, the issues concerning secular education have produced no apparent conflicts within the community. Except for the ultra-conservative element which demands the complete abolition of all secular material from the Yeshiva curriculum, the Satmar tolerate the presence of secular education, but at the same time discourage their children from actively participating in non-Jewish studies.[4]

In the Bobover community, a wide range of personal opinions has produced a situation that in some ways resembles Satmar, and in other ways conflicts radically with the policy of non-participation. As one student states, "It's the same Hasidus; we just emphasize different things." Below are four statements taken from individuals who are currently enrolled in the "English" program at the Bobover Yeshiva. They typify the attitudes found in the community at large.

> I don't care much for English. My English teacher is a Goy (non-Jew).[5] He doesn't even wear a beard. He doesn't have tsitsis. He takes from his head his hat when he leaves the Yeshiva. I don't even know if he eats Kosher. He's a goy. So what should I care about English taught by a goy....My father says better I should not learn English than lean from a goy. (11 years old)

> Learning English and division, subtraction, addition. These things are important. You need to know these things. But theories? Triangles? Protractors? History? What am I going to do with such things? We're not public school guys. We get up at six to learn two hours before eating even! It's crazy to think we have so much strength to sit and learn Torah all day and then this. I'm a Hasid; what I have to know I know from Torah and the Rebbe. For a job I'll need English and math, but not the other things they make you learn. It's useless. (Age 14)

> I think it's necessary to know how to read and write and also to have a sense of the laws and history of the United States. The ignorant are at the mercy of the informed. If we at least know the laws, we can protect ourselves. You don't have to believe. but you have to know. (Age 13)

> ...to make a living? If I'm smart enough I'll go to Kolel. Otherwise I'll go into some business. Diamonds is a good business. Who needs such junk litrich, algebara [sic]. (15 years old)

"This Yeshiva is one of the weaker ones where English is concerned," a member of the English faculty confided. "They allow it, they try to comply with the state regulations. It says something about opinions (concerning secular education) in the community." While many Yeshivas will submit to some form of secular regulation in order to qualify for state and federal funds, the Bobover administration makes an effort to create something more valid without offending the conservative elements who see no purpose in such endeavors. Material used in classes is carefully censored to conform with Hasidic beliefs and world view. Basic readers, for instance, which depict boys and girls holding hands or playing with animals are shunned in favor of adventure stories or fantasy tales. Teachers are hired for their cultural sympathies as well as academic qualifications. Accurate records of standard achievement tests are kept. Services such as speech therapy and remedial reading classes offered by the New York City school administration, are incorporated into the system too. Yet despite the honest effort made by the Yeshiva administration, the English program that theoretically culminates in a high school diploma is, as one administrator bluntly stated, "a failure after the eighth grade."

The cause for this failure cannot be attributed to any one predominant factor; no single reason exists. Rather the drastic attrition rate which occurs between the eighth and tenth grades results from several points of contention.

Formal instruction in the English program does not begin until a child is at least six years old. Classes are held four days a week from Monday through Thursday, for two hours each day. In the fourth grade, an additional half hour is added. From the seventh through twelfth grades, the instruction is offered in two forty-five minute periods; language and history are taught by one teacher, mathematics and science by another. Administration for the program functions semi-autonomously from the Yeshiva administration. There is a director, or principal for the primary grades one through eight, and another for the high school, grades nine through twelve. The principals and their assistants are responsible for determining curriculum, administering standardized tests, from Metropolitan Achievement Tests (MAT's) in the lower grades to New York State Regents Examinations in the high school. They are responsible for the generalities and details of the entire program. The Yeshiva administration is content to allow the two principals a free hand, for the most part, in the operation of their programs. The right to censor material and overrule certain decisions, however, is retained by Yeshiva authorities. Nevertheless, conflict between the two administrations is rare. Of the two men who currently oversee the English program, one is a respected Rabbi who teaches in the Bobover Mesivta, and the other is an Orthodox Jew, who sympathises with Hasidic beliefs and standards.

Teachers for the program are carefully selected. With rare exceptions, all secular instructors are either Hasidim or Orthodox Jews having a command of Yiddish. Although the students are encouraged to speak only English during class time, it is understood to be a point of comfort for both students and parents that even the English teachers are able to speak Yiddish. For many children, the two hours of secular instruction represent the only contact they have with non-Hasidic influences; the administration is loath to entrust the children to "contaminating" elements, especially at an early age. Another reason the Yeshiva tries to place sympathetic persons in secular positions is that of student cooperation. From the age of three, when a child first enters the Yeshiva environment, he is constantly reinforced to shun non-Hasidic elements; this applies to people as well as objects. Also, a denigrating attitude concerning secular studies evolves as a child progresses in his Hasidic education. Whatever benefit a child might gain from the limited secular education can easily be lost due to negative or hostile associations made by the child between the subject and the instructor. An instructor whom the child respects or identifies with, stands a far better chance of successfully imparting his lessons than an instructor who evokes neither response. Some positions, particularly in the areas of higher mathematics and science, are difficult to staff with acceptably observant Jews. In my observation of English classes, the contrasts between classes taught by Hasidim or Orthodox Jews and those taught by teachers from the outside were sharp. In one room, students sat obediently following the lessons; in the other, bedlam and general lack of cooperation characterized the forty minutes. Teaching under the latter, adverse condition is described as being "joyless and frustrating."

A child's interest in secular education decreases directly with his continual progress in Torah studies and community involvement. Enrollment and educational progress during the first six grades, measured by a series of standardized tests, remains constant. At this level, Jewish studies are still relatively generalized and conducted in a serious but relaxed atmosphere. Dress conformity is limited to the yamulka and talis katan. Parental control, rather than peer pressures, still exert the major influence over a child's behavior. Parents and administrators, aware that these first six school years might be the only opportunity for children to acquire a working knowledge of English, mathematics, and other secular information, try to take full advantage of the situation. The curriculum is heavily oriented towards reading, writing, and arithmetic. Lessons in history and geography double as reading exercises. Spelling and arithmetic tests are administered weekly. Tests are also given upon completion of each chapter of history and geography texts. Parents tend to be encouraging in these endeavors, within the limits imposed by their beliefs. While they will never order a child to forego their religious studies at home in favor of secular ones, they will insist on satisfactory completion of the required lessons, as evidenced by favorable school report cards. The English department also sponsors an "open school week," during which parents are urged to come and discuss their children's progress in secular studies. Sympathetic teachers are likely to minimize a boy's poor performance in English studies if he shows uncommon ability and progress in his Jewish classes. Students who show indifference or laziness in both curricula, however, are soundly reproached. Remedial reading and corrective speech therapy are used in conjunction with regular classes, for students in need of help in these areas. As in public schools, children with problems are given weekly appointments with the therapists. Students who are unusually adept at avoiding either therapy or remedial reading sessions are reprimanded and correctively disciplined by concerned Yeshiva teachers. Attendance is taken and noted with the same care as in the regular classes. Absence must be accompanied by an explanatory note from home; excessive absence results in a telephone call from the teacher.

Despite the general attitude that a secular education, beyond learning rudimentary skills, is irrelevant and even detrimental, many families (mothers particularly) express the desire that their sons complete the high school degree. The sons, of course, resist vigorously. Beginning with pre-Mesivta classes, when the pressures and status for becoming a Talmudic scholar intensify, performance in English classes deteriorates dramatically. "By the seventh or eighth grade, they're [the students] openly antagonistic to the idea of wasting time with English studies. Still, they do it, usually for another year, because of pressure from a parent." At this time, both Jewish and secular studies demand more of the student's time. More complex types of mathematics, such as algebra and geometry, are introduced into the program, along with history and literature. These require additional work at home. Meanwhile, the new world of the Bes Hamedresh is opening to the student; the peer group in the Mesivta also emerges at this time as the dominant force in the students' lives. The Bes Hamedresh is the realm of Torah and Hasidus; English is never heard during the endless observations and discourses of the Talmud chachamim or Talmudic scholars. Everywhere are signs of living Hasidus: studious, bearded faces; distinctive clothes; heavy books with cracked, worn covers. "It is no small wonder that <u>any</u> of them finish high school," a non-Hasidic teacher observed. "Who wants to be the one to walk into the study hall two hours after all your friends, with Pythagoras and rules for the correct use of the semicolon in your head?"

In order to drop out of the secular program, written permission from both parents must be obtained. In some cases this is not so easy. "You'll find the fathers easier to convince than the mothers," a teacher remarked. "A boy wants more time to devote to Torah; a father has been through it and incidentally gets some pride from a son who is noted for his learning, he comes up with his note pretty fast. But a woman sees things differently. She wants her son to be religious and a Talmud chacham, too, but she also maybe wants him to have a chance at a better job. She's harder to convince. Women think differently than men. It's to be expected." Since children are taught from infancy the importance of obeying the fifth Commandment, "Honor thy father and thy mother," total disregard of parental desires is unthinkable. But peer pressure and a personal distaste for secular materials weigh heavily upon the young scholars. In some cases, appealing to one's parents in the name of

Torah and Hasidus will produce the desired release from secular studies. If such a plea is consonant with either the family's scholastic or religious status, or the boy's individual development, the student need not apply any further pressure. The precious release note will be signed by both parents. Frequently, however, such tactics will evoke adamant refusals, especially if this "new-found holiness" seems to deviate from past behavior. In such cases, less subtle techniques are employed by the despairing boy. Some students will purposely refuse to participate in lessons, or will misbehave continuously in hopes that the ensuing embarrassment will compel the parents to withdraw him from English classes. Others will cut classes and miss exams until they reach the age of sixteen, when state law allows them to quit studies without parental permission. Sometimes, dismissal is granted by the administration, to avoid unpleasant conflicts. These are radical measures which often produce tension and discipline at home instead of the desired results.

In recent years, the International Correspondence School (ICS) has provided an agreeable solution for students and their parents. The correspondence course allows a boy to obtain a high school equivalency certificate through a home study program. "ICS leaves everyone happy here. Those boys who want a secular education, but object to the schedule or curriculum at the Yeshiva can complete their work in spare time and get a degree. Others take the course just to make the parents happy; they get a friend to do their tests. There is something for everyone. Students are happy, parents are happy; ICS gets paid, so they're happy, too."

Some families do not insist on securing a diploma; they are concerned only with the knowledge it represents. These families employ private tutors for their sons; in this way, they are able to control both the quality and content of the secular curriculum. Private tutors are expensive, though, and therefore do not constitute a viable alternative for any but the financially comfortable.

Although the secular educational facility has become a familiar component in the Bobover Yeshiva, it has not gained acceptance. Since its inception, the administration and instruction of the program have improved through experience. Texts have been upgraded. Despite this, only six students attending the twelfth grade were eligible for high school diplomas during the academic year 1974-75. Apparently, an avid desire to learn does not transcend cultural boundaries.

The most frequently heard complaint about the secular program is its irrelevancy to Hasidic life. "The boys here, even the most inquisitive, get all the intellectual stimulation they can handle from Torah. What they want, and don't get from the English program, are marketable skills, training that will make getting a job easier." In conjunction with the Federal government, the Yeshiva administers a job-training program that pays students to acquire various skills, such as typing and bus driving. But the program's limitations are obvious: there are not too many positions available within the community for typists and school bus drivers.

As residents of New York City, Hasidim are eligible to attend any of the tuition-free City University colleges. Social and accredition factors inhibit their utilization of this opportunity. "We cannot send our children to places where the social situation is lacking in morals, and the only way to get a degree is to take subjects which contradict our beliefs and teachings. Certain subjects such as business or pure mathematics, there's nothing wrong with that. But to get a degree you have to study other things too."

Footnotes - Appendix I

1. Lucy S. Dawidowicz, *The Golden Tradition*, Beacon Press, Boston, 1966, p. 30.

2. Dawidowicz, p. 31.

3. Dawidowicz. p. 31.

4. Rubin, p. 149.

5. This, in fact, is not true. The Bobover hire only Jewish teachers. What the information is referring to is the fact that the teacher is not an observant Jew.

APPENDIX II

The main drawback to collecting data through observation and key man interview methods, is the limitation on the number of people to whom one can talk. In a population the size of the Bobover Yeshiva, it is a physical impossibility to interview everyone. And yet, there were questions and facts which could not be corroborated merely by dealing with a representative segment of the Yeshiva population. To broaden the scope of the inquiry, a questionnaire was developed which was administered to two hundred students between the ages of nine and eighteen. The questionnaire, which was censored by the administration, was designed to elicit general information in three areas:

(1) Personal data--which produced an accurate accounting of family units; where siblings attended school, or lived; occupation of parents; country of origin.

(2) Extracurricular activities and general environment--since it was obvious that the Yeshiva exerted the greatest influence in a child's life, I was curious about the extent to which they were affected by the outside environment. Did they have non-Hasidic acquaintances? Did they travel outside the community? How did this affect their ideational

perceptions? Were they really as insular as they seemed to be?

(3) <u>Occupational and marital expectations and preconceptions</u>--since young men are theoretically not supposed to be concerned with matrimonial pursuits, many questions I submitted were unacceptable and those that were included in the questionnaire were often left blank or answered "I don't know." Occupational responses showed a predictable conformity.

The questionnaire was helpful in that it provided a means for reaching a larger proportion of the student population. Through the questionnaire, I was able to see far beyond the boundaries of the Yeshiva walls, into homes and family groups to see who spent how much time doing what and where. Also, it was possible to determine patterns of settlement of both parents and their married children. The answers to certain questions dispelled several misconceptions I had harbored from the outset of the project. I assumed that in order to insulate their children, the Bobover denied them access to the world outside. For an "insulated" group, the children proved to be well-travelled, if not well-informed by today's standards.[1] Of course, travel was restricted between point of departure and point of arrival, but the sights in between were duly noticed. The questionnaire as an object in itself, showed to what degree the

Bobover children have accepted a knowledge of English as necessary and pertinent to their lives. The questionnaire was written in English. The ability to read and express one's thoughts in, what to many is a second language, reinforced the information collected on secular learning.

The major limitation in the use of a questionnaire was the circumstances under which it was administered. The Yeshiva administration insisted that the only time such behavior would be tolerated was during the English class hours. Religious instruction could never be interrupted for things of this nature. The administration felt that reading the questions and writing answers could be considered as a lesson--in reading and writing. The development of time in which the questionnaire was administered effectively skewed any balanced conclusions one could derive from the raw data. Since attendance in English classes falls off rapidly after the eighth grade (fourteen year olds) the number of completed questionnaires from young men between the ages of fifteen and nineteen is insignificant and cannot be considered representative in any category.[2]

Footnotes - Appendix II

1. The three most common places for youngsters to have travelled are Israel, London, Belgium--all of which have Bobover communities.

2. Plagiarism, if the word applies to the situation, was prevalent in all age groups. Whether it reflected an unwillingness to cooperate with a project similar to Standardized Testing, which most children scorn, or a poor command of the English language remains undetermined. Several questionnaires in each group were identical, misspelled word for misspelled word.

GENEALOGY

I. DISCIPLES

    Baal Shem Tov (ca. 1700-1760)

    Dov Baer, The Maggid of Mezeritch (1704-1772)

    Elimelekh of Lizensk (1717-1786)

    Naftali of Ropshitz (1740-1809)

    Chaim Halberstam of Sanz (1792-1875)

II. BOBOVER DYNASTY

    Chaim Halberstam of Sanz

    Shlomo Halberstam (grandson)
    the first Bobover Rebbe (1846-1905)

    Ben Zion Halberstam (son)
    the second Bobover Rebbe (1872-1941)

    Shlomo Halberstam (son)
    the present Bobover Rebbe

GLOSSARY

Key to Pronounciation

a - a as in palm	o - o as in bold
e - e as in end	oy-oi as in poise
ay- a as in late	u -oo as in noon
i - i as in pity	ch-ch as in German ach
	s - s as in soon

Bar Mitzvah (Hebrew)	– Literally, son of the commandment. The initiation of a Jewish male child into adulthood at the age of 13
Bes Hamedresh (Bes Medresh) (Hebrew)	– Place for religious services or study
Bekesher (Yiddish)	– A long Hasidic coat made of silk or silken material
Chassanah (Hebrew)	– Wedding
Chayder (Hebrew)	– Elementary religious school
Chazer (Yiddish)	– Literally, to repeat
Chumesh (Hebrew)	– Pentateuch or Five Books of Moses
Chuppa (Hebrew)	– Wedding canopy
Chusan (Hebrew)	– A bridegroom
Colla (Hebrew)	– A bride
Davn (Yiddish)	– To pray
Frum (Yiddish)	– Pious
Gartl (Yiddish)	– A woven silk belt worn during prayer

Goy (Hebrew)	– Gentile
Gemorah (Hebrew)	– Part of the Talmud which consists of the interpretation and discussion of the law as presented in the Mishna
Hasid (Hebrew or Yiddish)	– Literally, pious one. A follower or member of the Hasidic movement
Ibitseer (Yiddish)	– Long coat. Worn in place of suit jacket
Kapota (Yiddish)	– A long overcoat
Kosher (Hebrew)	– Ritually fit to use. Food prepared according to the dietary laws
Kvitl (Yiddish)	– Note. A written request presented to a Hasidic leader
Mazel Tov (Hebrew)	– Good luck
Mashgiach (Hebrew)	– Supervisor. An overseer of religious matters
Meshiach (Hebrew)	– Messiah
Mikva (Hebrew)	– Ritual bath for purification
Mishna (Hebrew)	– Literally, oral study. The collection of laws upon which the Talmud is based
Mitzvah (Hebrew)	– Divine commandment; good deed; merit
Morah (Hebrew)	– Teacher
Nigun (Hebrew)	– Melody or tune
Parsha (Hebrew)	– Portion of the Five Books of Moses
Peyes (Hebrew)	– Earlocks
Purim (Hebrew)	– Holiday commemorating the defeat of Haman described in the Book of Esther

Rebbe (Hebrew)	– Teacher. Title of a Hasidic leader
Rebbetzen (Hebrew)	– Wife of a Rabbi or Rebbe
Rov (Hebrew)	– Rabbi. A religious leader of a Jewish congregation ordained by well-known religious scholars. An expert on all points of Jewish law and the ultimate authority in conflicts concerning interpretation of the law
Samat (Yiddish)	– Velvet
Sefer (Hebrew)	– Books in Hebrew with a religious content
Shabbos (Hebrew)	– Sabbath
Shadchen (Yiddish)	– Matchmaker or marriage broker
Sheer (Hebrew)	– Lecture
Sheytl (Yiddish)	– Wig
Shidach (Hebrew)	– A match or marriage
Shteibl (Yiddish)	– Small prayer room
Shtreiml (Yiddish)	– A hat made of sable or other costly fur
Shtetl (Yiddish)	– Small town or village
Talis (Hebrew)	– Literally, small prayer shawl. A ritual undergarment worn by Orthodox male Jews
Talmud (Hebrew)	– The basic body of Jewish oral law consisting of the interpretation of laws contained in the Torah
Talmud Chacham (Hebrew)	– A learned man

Tefillin (Hebrew)	– Phylacteries. Leather cases containing quotations from the Pentateuch, worn by Jews on the forehead and on the left arm during morning prayer.
T'noyim (Hebrew)	– Marriage contract
Torah (Hebrew)	– The teachings. The law. The Old Testament. The entire body of Jewish wisdom
Tzaddik (Hebrew)	– The Saint. The righteous. A Hasidic leader.
Tziduka (Hebrew)	– Charity
Yarmulka (Hebrew)	– Skull cap
Yeshiva (Hebrew)	– A religious school. A rabbinical academy
Yichus (Hebrew)	– Lineage
Yid (Yiddish)	– Jew
Yiddish (Yiddish)	– Jewish. In Jewish language
Yiddishkeit (Yiddish)	– Jewishness. Jewish way of life
Yontef (Yiddish)	– Holiday

BIBLIOGRAPHY

Articles

Gersh, Harry and Sam Miller, "Satmar in Brooklyn," Commentary 28; 389-999, 1959

Maccoby, Eleanore E. and Nathan Maccoby, "The Interview: A Tool of Social Science," in Gardener Lindzey (ed.), Handbook of Social Psychology, Vol. I (Reading, Mass.: Addison Wesley Publishing Co., Inc., 1954)

Paul, Benjamin D., "Interview Techniques and Field Relationships," in Alfred Kroeber (ed.), Anthropology Today (Chicago: University of Chicago Press, 1953)

Rabinovich, Wolf, "Karlin Hasidism," YIVO Annual of Jewish Social Sciences, 123-151, 1950.

Zborowski, Mark, "The Place of Book Learning in Traditional Jewish Culture," Harvard Educational Review XIY, 2:83-109, 1949.

Books

Buber, Martin. The Origin and Meaning of Hasidism. New York: Horizon Press, 1960.

Dawidowicz, Lucy S. The Golden Tradition. Boston: Beacon Press, 1967.

Herzog, Elizabeth and Mark Zborowski. Life Is With People. New York: Schocken Press, 1952.

Hostetter, John A. and Gertrude E. Huntington. Children in Amish Society. New York: Holt, Rinehart and Winston, 1971.

Pertti, Pelto. Anthropological Research: The Structure of Inquiry. New York: Harper and Row, 1970.

Rabinowicz, H. A Guide to Hasidism. London and New York: T. Yoseloff, 1960.

Rubin, Israel. *Satmar: An Island in the City*. Chicago: Quadrangle Books, 1972.

Scholom, Gershon. *Major Trends in Jewish Mysticism*. New York: Schocken Books, 1941.

INDEX

America (see United States)
Amish - 21, 22
Asceticism - 83, 84
Assimilation -
   fear of - 20
   methods for combating - 22, 27, 29
   reactions to - 27, 55

Bar mitzvah -
   significance - 76
Bekesher - 26, 70, 87
Belgium - 20
Beth Jacob - 49
Bobov - 6, 32
Bobover Rebbe -
   immigration to New York - 24
   relation to community - 24, 25, 32, 27-41, 52, 57, 76, 97, 104
   settlement in Boro Park - 24, 26

Canada - 32
Career -
   limitations - 95-104
   objectives - 95-104
   opportunities - 95-104
   preparations - 95-104
   restrictions - 95-104
Chanukah - 46, 51
Charity - 102, 104
Chayder - 34
   curriculum - 58-62
Chazer - 65-66, 74
Chuppa - 14
Chusan - 93, 95, 105
Colla - 96
Crown Heights - 24, 25-26
Crown School - 110

Dance -
   at wedding - 14, 16
Davn (see prayer)
Diamond Exchange - 68, 103
Dov Baer - 2

Dress -
    conformity - 44, 78, 86-88
    deviation - 87-88, 90
    form 87-88
    function - 27-28, 88

Education -
    curriculum - 43-50, 58-62, 67, 70-71, 85-86
    for females - 49-50, 54
    methodology - 43-50, 65-68, 74
    non-religious (see English)
    structure of system - 7, 55-57, 75, 84, 86
    summer program - 35, 50
Egypt - 43
Employment -
    see career
Engagement -
    description of - 97
England - 20
Enlightenment -
    effect on Hasidism - 89
English - 34
    attitude toward learning 34-35, 111-114, 116-117, 118, 121
    curriculum - 113, 116, 118
        use of - 44, 115, 118
Europe - 1, 20, 24, 32, 54, 83

Galicia - 6, 19, 24, 89-90
Games
    (see sports)
Gemorah - 50, 67, 78
Germantown - 21

Hagadah
    use in school - 60
Halakha -
    (see Farah)
Halberstam - 24
    Benzion - 24
    Shlomo - 24
Hasidim -
    (see Bobov, Bobover)
Hasidism -
    belief system of - 3-5
    history of - 1-4, 19-21
Holidays -
    relation to education - 46, 51, 58-62
Hungary - 6, 19
Hutterites - 22, 27

Ibitseer - 87, 96

Identity
    elements composing - 42, 43
    through dress - 42 (see dress)
    with community - 52, 95
    with peer group - 69, 72, 77-83
    with Rebbe - 36-42
International Correspondence School - 120-121
Iowa - 21
Israel -
    identity with - 2-5
    travel to - 32, 84
Israel Baalshem Tov - 2,4

Kapota - 13
Kessler, Rabbi Moishe - 9-10
Kindergarten - 48, 58
Kolel - 101, 102

London - 24, 84

Marriage -
    broker - (see shadchen)
    celebration, description of - 13-18
    contract - 97
    proper age for - 27, 93
    Purpose - 18-19, 93
Mashgiach - 85, 96
Megilla -
    use in school - 60
Mennonites - 21, 22
Mesivta - 76-87
Metropolitan Achievement Tests - 114
Mikva - 78
Minyan - 80
    bochim minyan - 81
Mintz, Jerome - 52
Molokans - 21
Mount Sinai - 3-5, 7
Music -
    at home - 52-53
    in celebration - 14, 16, 52
    in prayer - 59
    in school - 43

New England - 20
New Jersey - 84
New York City - 1, 18, 20, 22

Nigunim - 32-54
Nursery School - 36, 38
   form - 42-43
   function - 43-48

Ohio - 21

Palestine - 19
Passover - 51, 60
   (also see Holidays)
Pennsylvania - 21
Peyes - 11, 36, 38, 42
   (also see Identity)
Phonograph - 53
Pilgrims - 20
Poland - 6, 19, 24, 89-90
Prayer - 33, 35
   in community - 63
   in education - 51, 58, 63-65
Purim - 46, 51
   (also see Holidays)
Puritans - 20

Questionnaire - 124
   Hasidic response to - 126
   research tool - 10-11, 125-126

Rashi - 67
Rebbe - 2-3, 32-33
   (also see Bobover)
Rebbetzen - 39
Rash Yeshiva - 85
Rov - (see Bobover)
Russia - 110

Samat kepelish - 87
Satmar - 111
Shadchen -
   function - 95
   types of - 96
Sheer - 78, 85
Shevas Baruchas - 17
Sheytl - 14
Shteibl - 26, 81
Shtreiml - 11, 26, 37
Simchas Torah - 56
Skvira - 22
   skverer Hasidim - 22
Sports -
   participation in - 50, 70
   resistance to - 51, 70

Spring Valley - 22

Talis - 18, 38-39, 41
Talis Katan - 40, 42, 116
Talmud - 4
Teachers -
   female - 48-49
   objectives - 50
   male - 49, 58, 65, 71
   relation to community - 49, 71
   relation to students - 78
Teffilin - 76
Tish - 53. 57
Torah -
   definition of - 2-5, 28-29
   reading of - 61, 66
   transcription of - 28
Travel - 32, 84
Tzaddik - 2-3

United States - 6, 20, 29, 54

Williamsburg - 5, 26
World War II -
   Hasidic experience during - 82
   Hasidic experience after - 19-20

Yarmulka - 23, 36, 38, 42, 86, 116
Yichus - 39
Yiddish
   in education - 44, 47, 48
   use of - 26, 44, 49
Yiddishkeit